BEYOND PULPIT, CLASSROOM and LECTURE HALL

Unlocking Exposition, Instruction
and Research Reporting
in Subject Matter Sharing

Hollis L. Green

GlobalEdAdvance
Press

BEYOND PULPIT, CLASSROOM AND LECTURE HALL
UNLOCKING EXPOSITION, INSTRUCTION AND RESEARCH
REPORTING IN SUBJECT MATTER SHARING

Copyright © 2021 by Hollis L. Green

Library of Congress Control Number: 2020925248

ISBN 978-1-950839-03-2

Hollis Lynn Green 1933 -

Subject Codes and Description: 1. Religion/General; 2. Education/General; 3. Language Arts & Disciplines/Communication Studies

All rights reserved, including the right to reproduce this book or any part thereof in any form, except for inclusion of brief quotations in a review, without the written permission of GlobalEdAdvancePRESS and the author. Old Testament scriptures not otherwise noted are from the NIV. New Testament scriptures are primarily from EDNT unless otherwise noted.

Cover by GlobalGraphicsNYC

City of Publication: Nashville, TN

Printed in Australia, Brazil, EU, France, Germany, Italy, Poland, Russia, Spain, UK (3 sites in USA) and available on the Espresso Book Machine© worldwide.

The Press does not have ownership of the contents of a book; this is the author's work and the author owns the copyright. All theory, concepts, constructs, and perspectives are those of the author and not necessarily the Press. They are presented for open and free discussion of the issues involved. All comments and feedback should be directed to the Email: [comments4author@aol.com] and the comments will be forwarded to the author for response.

Order books from www.gea-books.com/bookstore/

or any place good books are sold.

Published by

GlobalEdAdvancePRESS

www.gea-books.com

DEDICATION

This work is affectionally dedicated to

PAUL F. HENSON

A man who loved His God, sacred music, And the written Word.

Each audience he faced was blessed with an Inspirational song and a warm message.

All who heard him sing or speak were Attracted by his voice and attached to His heart. His love for God and people Were present in each song and especially In his warm pulpit homily of Love and Grace! Paul was a treasured friend and a Magnificent preacher.

> "Love takes up
> where knowledge leaves off."
>
> (Thomas Aquinas)

Contents

Author's Preface		9
Introduction		15
Chapter 1	RESOURCES AND RESTRICTIONS	19
Chapter 2	COMPLEXITY AND VAGUENESS	29
Chapter 3	DIRECTION AND GUIDANCE	49
Chapter 4	LISTENING AND LEARNING	67
Chapter 5	MESSAGE AND DIALOGUE	87
Chapter 6	SHARING AND KNOWLEDGE	105
Chapter 7	PULPIT AND CLASSROOM	127
Chapter 8	PREPARATION AND DELIVERY	147
Chapter 9	SPEECH AND COMMUNICATION	169
Chapter 10	CONGREGANTS AND EDUCATION	185
Chapter 11	RESEARCH AND REPORTING	205
Chapter 12	CRITICAL THINKING AND DISCOVERY	219
About The Author		227
Afterword		229
Appendix A — Survey Form		232
Results Of Survey		234
Summary Report		235
Appendix B		237
Appendix C		243
Appendix D		276
Bibliography		280

The intent and function of sharing data, information, or facts by speaker and location may be the only definable differences together with many similarities.

Author's Preface

Subject Matter Sharing

Once the title of this book is read, the logical question is "beyond what?" Beyond the credentials and certification of the speaker is the integrity and character of the presenter apart from the functional duties of the position. A value judgement by the listener, as to the moral authority, character and authenticity of the presenter, is a value assigned to the language and structure of the performance. The logical questions by the audience are: who are you, why are you here, what qualifies you to speak on the subject at hand? Beyond the subject matter sharing is the person, their position, personality and preparation for the occasion.

Performance magnifies character and multiple exposure unwraps layers of personality, integrity, temperament and moral fiber of the presenter. The reason the individuals are present either adds or subtracts from the value of subject matter exposure. Certainly, one may learn "something" from a poorly written book, a teacher not fully prepared, or a minister who displays too much raw human nature. Nevertheless, the advance preparation of the presenter may determine both the attentiveness of the audience and the quality of learning and application of the subject content.

These are some of the essential elements used by participants to attribute value to the subject matter shared by a particular person. They suggest to the listener possible behavior of the speaker apart from their functional duties. When a speaker is *"in character for a performance,"* but would rather be somewhere else, attentive listeners are aware of the duplicity. Most of the general public have heard about an immoral minister, ghost writers for known celebrities, a family man who takes advantage of an employer's trust for personal gain, a weak teacher who cannot leave their personal problems outside the classroom, or an author who intentionally plagiarizes the work of others. These known facts impact the assessment of a speaker by the audience. Nonetheless, mature listeners have the capacity to glean from a presentation both concepts and constructs that are useful additions to their knowledge base.

There are no wide-ranging differences in subject matter sharing whether from a pulpit, a classroom or lecture hall, except the audience assessment of the character and integrity of the speaker. The objectives are clear: accurate and detailed communication. The intent and function of sharing data, information, or facts by speaker and location may be the only definable differences together with similarities. The speaker must have advance preparation, focus on the venue, and have broad knowledge of the subject matter. Human activities within the social professions are not easily divided into secular, sacred and scholarly. On the other hand, the audience will make assessments as to the worth of content and the veracity of the speaker based on subjective criteria. Consequently, the moral character and personality of the presenter may equal the value with all the other qualifications.

Teachers serve a noble profession and are considered secular and neutral; clergymen are judged to be sacred and sectarian, and those reporting research are seen as academic and scholarly. Nonetheless, behavior and performance are not apparent from fixed predispositions or evident lifestyles. Subject matter sharing may be classified by intention and delivery or generalized by location, speaker, or subject matter, but principles and methods by which data are transferred are standard and related to communication theory. All this will be analyzed and valued by the listener and weighed against the presentation of content.

Excitement of discovery comes early in education. My earliest memory of a caring and guiding force outside my family and church, was my Fifth Grade Teacher, Lea Hudson Hoodenpyle, who taught me the excitement of discovery and pointed me toward lifelong learning. It was my privilege to dedicate one of my best-selling books: *Transformational Leadership in Education – A Strengths-based approach to change for Administrator, Teachers & Guidance Counselors* to honor her. It was a privilege to attend her funeral and thank her children for the early educational guidance from their mother. Such efforts should always be remembered by those who benefit from the sacrificial service of others. Memory of those who provided early direction and guidance is an obvious part of the maturing process.

Weight and substance of a sanctuary homily may depend on both visual and memory connotations. Significance may hinge on the sectarian position of the group, the personality of the speaker, or the day of the week. There are always subtexts, overtones, and hidden agendas that influence both speaker and listener and weight the worth of words. The quality of the lesson plan, the teacher's manner, and the advance preparation of the class all impact the value of the outcome of class-based learning. The delivery impact from a lectern depends on the subject, venue, speaker and the nature of the occasion. The reading of an academic paper, the report of new research, the introduction of a new book, or a studied speech on a critical subject, all influence how the listener weighs the substance of the subject and/or makes an application of the content. Value of content transfer depends on prior awareness of the subject, informed participation and the audience assessment of the speaker.

The meaning assigned to a classroom subject may depend on the instructor, the content and context of the course, and the personal stake a learner may have in the outcome. Does the teacher stimulate interest in the subject and arouse a spirit of inquiry by the listener? Does the content have apparent value for an upcoming examination? Is the subject matter considered essential to the course of study? May what is learned be applied to life and/or career? The big questions are: is the teacher prepared and believable, the information beneficial, and are the participants informed by prior knowledge and advance preparation? And of course, is the subject required or an elective?

Career guidance normally comes from a seasoned professional. One afternoon, Col. Creed Bates called me to his office for sound counsel that shaped a large part of my life. He said, *"I understand you do not plan to make the military your career and that you prefer to work with people in some form of ministry. Don't think that 4 years of college and 3 years of seminary will qualify you to communicate with anyone. You must work with people full time and go to school part-time and learn to share what you were taught with others as you learn."* What happened to all the honest and forthright advisors of young people? They are needed for each generation!

With this guidance and no present funds for further education, my decision was to continue my activities with young people and share what had already been learned. Col. Bates' advice made me aware of my need for both practical experience and formal education. It was sound advice and fit into my limited budget for formal education and the opportunity to continue working with young people to gain practical experience.

Continuing to follow the advice of Col. Bates, my task was to work with young people, work with small churches, initiate youth programs and enroll in classes as opportunity and funds were available. After years of academic struggle to acquire a quality education, in 2007, it was an honor to dedicate my book, *Sympathetic Leadership Cybernetics –serving individuals in groups, and/or organizations* to Col. Bates, as an advisor who influenced my professional life and practical service through education.

The urgency of my specific call seemed to be sidetracked or temporarily slowed by blocks of time spent in formal studies, serving local pastorates, a Reserve Chaplain during the Vietnam era, and bi-vocational endeavors. However, in the process, valued learning and relevant experience were gained that would impact future academic administration, leadership, seminary and graduate school professorships. Time and opportunity pushed me toward teaching, writing books, and traveling as an educational missionary. With the public speaking, teaching, and sharing in faith-based venues, my primary vocation has been sharing in the classroom and by writing books. This book, while pushing age 87, becomes #56 in my list of published works in support of my ministry through education.

    Hollis L. Green, ThD, PhD, DLitt
    The Evergreen Cottage
    Morning Air Estate on Lone Mountain
    37321-7635 Tennessee USA

    Fall of 2020

Introduction

Commonalities vs. Differences

*Differences divide but
Commonalities unite!*

After decades of preaching, teaching and reporting the findings of social research, it appears there is no significant difference in the process of subject matter sharing whether from a pulpit, a classroom, a lecture hall, or a published manuscript. The objectives are clear: accurate and detailed communication. The intent and function of sharing data, information, or facts by speaker and location may be the only definable differences together with many similarities. The speaker's advance preparation must provide comprehensive knowledge of the subject matter, together with a focus on the audience and venue.

The common-sense key to listening and learning is *"respect."* An unabridged dictionary defines respect *'look at and pay attention to."* Respect for yourself, the subject matter, and the speaker using common words to reach the audience becomes the door to significant learning. Speakers and listeners must use their common sense in dealing with the sharing of quality and quantity of existing and accessible subject matter.

Teachers serve a noble profession and are considered secular and neutral; clergymen are judged to be sacred and sectarian; those reporting research are academic and scholarly. However, behavior and performance are not apparent from fixed predispositions or evident lifestyles. Subject matter sharing may be classified by intention and delivery or generalized by location, speaker, subject matter, but principles and methods by which data are transferred are standard and related to communication theory.

The sharing/learning process in conveying subject matter can best be explained by a connection with those desiring to nurture others or deal with problems which impact real life situations. The action steps taken to nurture growth and address the problems of life by sharing relevant subject matter, whether the spokesperson is a parent, friend or mentor, the intent to transfer valued information or specific guidance which may be used to increase the knowledge base has commonalties. The sharing and learning process is similar whether the information is shared in a sacred sanctuary, a public classroom or new findings reported in a book or presented in an academic lecture hall. Although intention is a primary indicator that differentiate secular, sacred and scholarly, some may attribute different forms of influence to subject matter sharing.

Research is personal discovery and a snapshot of findings and some may issue a false claim unintentionally. A few may still believe Columbus discovered America! He did not live to be embarrassed, but with current technology any absent-minded effort may be exposed even if it were unintentional.

My earliest memory of learning came when some perspective or understanding came fresh to me. At the moment, it was considered a "new discovery" made by me apart from all others. Of course, it was just the joy and excitement of learning from a good teacher. Later, when a significant insight came, as a result of study or research, it was a spiritual experience. Then when social scientific research methodology and statistics became a part of my studies, true personal discovery became possible. When valid research assumptions on a known problem were structured and hypothesized assertions were tested by the appropriate statistical procedures, the findings were "new data" indeed. *Eureka* - a sudden triumphant discovery!

Sure, someone else could follow a similar research path and discover the same reality, but both the excitement of first discovery and then the realization that others would follow became a head clearing event. Another awareness was that new knowledge came with the assistance of many teachers from past education and reading which paved the way forward. It was time to *"pay it forward."* Those who learn must also teach others!

Later, upon learning that the Greeks had two words for knowledge, my excitement was directed toward deeper study of semantics in linguistic changes in the meaning of individual words and concepts. From one perspective, the Greek "gnosis" knowledge came from *books and teachers*, but the other construct was "epignoseos" for *full knowledge that came from personal experience* and/or investigative endeavors that produced first-hand experiential knowledge. That one could learn educationally and spiritually through processing personal experience was encouraging.

When something was learned from an answered prayer or from using statistics to test hypotheses that produced valid findings, it was a fresh discovery.

Learning through experiential discovery was exciting. Doing social research became a new way to generate specialized knowledge and experience the thrill of breakthrough discovery. The reporting and sharing of research findings became a passion to share past experience and learning. Hopefully, it will become part of my academic legacy.

Chapter 1

Resources and Restrictions

*Surrogate nurturing is a vital part
of growing up.*

Providence normally arranges resources from family and friends which provide early guidance toward a career path. Along the journey, common sense and the circumstances of life provide resources, restrictions, and opportunities for education and guidance to keep one on track. Early guidance for my calling and ultimate ministry through education came from various sources. My father passed three months before my fifth birthday. Mother was left with three small children: a girl 9, me, and a baby just 6 months old. She was a schoolteacher and sang in the church choir and taught an adult Bible Class. Her concern *"What am I going to do with a growing boy during Sunday services?"* This was before church programming separated children from the sanctuary worship and they missed the lessons learned from pastoral guidance.

Surrogate nurturing is a vital part of growing up. On a Sunday morning following my father's passing, mother took the family to church. Two men, Ira and Lester Johnson, who had no kinship, but shared a common interest in children, came to mother and asked, *"Mrs. Green, if you don't mind, we will take charge of Hollis during the service?"* Mother's prayers were answered, and she could teach the class and sing in the choir without concerns as to the mischief her son may create. *[It would have been a tragic loss to my upbringing had I missed the pastoral message and God's Guiding Hand from Ira and Lester Johnson as they provided surrogate watch care for me.]*

Reality checks are required as one grows. One of my earliest memories was my desire to be properly dressed at all times. Mother had cut down one of my father's suits for his funeral. Feeling like a man in a three-piece suit, but reality ruled the day: the underclothes, socks and shoes were those of a little boy on his way to his father's funeral. Growing up does have reality checks built into the living system. There are things we all must learn or suffer grievous consequences. To this day Ira and Lester Johnson are remembered for their concern for a young boy without a father's guidance during the growing years.

Specific instructions from friends and family are of great value to the young. Ira and Lester Johnson, with a gentle hand and soft voice instructed me where to sit during Sunday worship and to go to the bathroom and get a drink of water before the service began and not to move from my seat until the final *"Amen!"* Usually, one of the men sat behind me on the second pew with me on the first pew at the end. My instructions were to pay attention, listen to the songs and the sermon. The pew had a nice curved end and I learned to prop my arm on the end piece and put my hand under my chin and take a nap looking straight at the pulpit. At least there was quietness and I was learning the value of good behavior during a religious service.

The value of listening should be learned early in life. My restriction of movement was a clear lesson in listening. Through the next few years, my interest in what the pastor was saying about God and Jesus became of interest. As a child without a father or brother, to learn that God was my Father and that Jesus was my big Brother was most encouraging. At age 9, my Sunday school class (ages 9 -11) elected me class President and Bible study became serious business. We had a teacher who was not always present and by default the responsibility to teach the lesson fell on me. You see, my mother was a schoolteacher and there was little n a widow's house to entertain children in those days. Mother required me and my older sister to prepare to be *"informed participants"* in class. This is why at age 12, the class elected me as their teacher. Thank God for a teaching mother and for Ira and Lester Johnson who took an interest in me and exercised *"spiritual adoption"* to do basic watch care and guidance in church during my early years. My experience was much better than the present system, where children are shuffled off to Children's Church, and miss hearing the anointed homily of a loving pastor.

Special agenda meetings were a rare event in the church of my youth. At age 12, the pastor announced a special agenda meeting for tithe paying male members only. Since I was a male member who tithed income from using my red wagon to pull groceries home for the elderly, my eligibility was assured. The meeting was placed on my limited schedule. As soon as the pastor arrived for the meeting, he thought it not good for a young boy to be present because they were to discuss some behavioral matters about two church leaders. Both Johnson men stood, *"This young man will be a church leader someday and he should learn both sides of the story."* Then several other men expressed the desire for me to stay. Perhaps my youthful ears were not ready to hear about *hanky-panky* between the music director and the piano player, but thinking it was non-church music, the fuss seemed over blown.

The men standing up for me taught a valuable lesson. Yes, something about the other side of the situation was learned. Later, understanding that hanky-panky was dubious behavior of a sexual nature and considered improper by the church, a good lesson had been learned for my future teaching/preaching endeavors.

At age 14, asked to speak at a youth service in a small rural church was a start. The next Sunday my pastor developed bronchiectasis (called Preacher's croup in the non-airconditioned days) and asked me to speak to about 300 folks in the evening service. After the meeting, Lester Johnson came to mother, *"Mrs. Green, if it is OK with you, Ira and I would like to buy Hollis a preaching suit."* The Johnson suit was my second suit and was worn with pride for my first studio picture. My first suit was made from my father's best 3-piece Sunday deacon suit in time for his funeral. Mother cut the suit, white shirt, tie and belt down to my size. Dressed me for the service and said, *"You are now the man of the house, and in the future I will consult you on major decisions I must make about our family."*

Orphan girls and poor boys without a father's care need surrogate guidance. In fact, the Johnsons' love for children was further demonstrated when, as married men without children, they adopted two sisters and each one raised one, but kept them together as sisters in church, school and in a family relationship. God bless such men who care for orphan girls and poor boys without a father's care. This is what the Bible called *"pure religion"* and I am confident that God has a special place in heaven for such people. Families, faith-based groups and the world would be much better if there were more teaching mothers and churchmen with a *"father's heart"* filled with a Divine Nurturing Attribute (DNA) that comes with a deep and abiding spiritual relationship with God. There is a need for spiritual adoption of the young without the watch care of a father. Both men and women willing to serve as remedial and surrogate parents* for the young are needed to assist growing learners and future leaders.

---

*Recommended reading; *Remedial and Surrogate Parenting: A Resource for Parents, Teachers and Child Care Services* (2013) Hollis L.Green, ISBN 978-1-9354344-81--Children are a gift of God and a legacy of faith-based families; therefore, parenting skills are an essential aspect of human development. This work is guidance for remedial human development (0-20) for parents, teachers, and childcare workers.

(www.gea-books.com)

The local Church Council asked me to serve as Youth Leader during my last year of high school, this encouraged me on an early career path. The youth leaders initiated a Saturday evening service to rally young people of the community and managed to attract a good crowd on Saturday night with the youth in charge.

With no present funds for college, the first weekend after graduation, began a travel schedule for youth meetings in Arkansas, Alabama and West Virginia. God was with me and so was Mother's Bible and the Johnson preaching suit. It was the beginning of a long journey. My first attempt at speaking for a youth meeting outside of Tennessee was in Bald Knob, Arkansas.

Traveling by train all night from Chattanooga, there were stops at every local station before arriving at Bald Knob station about 9 AM on Sunday. Tired but not wanting to be late, a taxi was taken to the local church. It was a church much larger than expected. Meeting the pastor, he was kind but said, *"Son, the taxi brought you to the wrong church, let me drive you to the other side of town to the church where you are supposed to be."* Arriving at a small church with about 60 people and no young folk. Disappointed but pleased to have an opportunity to speak. That was the beginning of a long traveling and speaking journey to more than 100 countries.

Considering myself a New Testament Christian, not tied to a particular sectarian position, opened many doors to share my faith-based ministry of encouragement.

Speaking at a youth meeting in Alabama, Max Morris, a young pianist, offered to take me to see an old preacher and his special dog. Arriving, the old preacher said, *"You came to see my dog, didn't you?"* He took us straight to his main dog and said, *"I call this dog, 'Moreover.' His name comes from the Bible... over there where 'Moreover' the dog came and licked the sores of Lazarus."* **A name for a dog from sacred scripture was a stretch, but it was the old preacher's means to share a message.** He no longer had a pulpit, but he still had a message to share with anyone who would listen. The visit to the old preacher sparked a realization that God can use anyone or anything to deliver His message: a donkey, rocks to praise Him, or the wind in a Mulberry tree to send a message. Why not an old preacher's dog to point people to a sacred scripture?

My conclusion after 65 years of active ministry through education and lifestyle, the world needs more teaching mothers and more churchmen who care for children the way Ira and Lester Johnson demonstrated concern for me and others without a father's guidance. Local churches need more men who see potential in the young and the field of education could use a few more teachers with moral and ethical concern to share fact-based truth with students. Such individuals become participants in *"pure religion"* which is transparent in their behavior toward others. Those whom God calls in their youth are qualified by upbringing, life experience, wise counsel, and educational opportunities. It is a blessing to have the pull and push of a call to participate with others on a shared journey to develop moral excellence in yourself and others.

Perhaps this is why we see so many young ministers doing well and both young men and women teaching at the University level. They are closer to the culture and the point of learning the subject matter they wish to share. They have a *"first generation perspective"* and use understandable language and examples. This gives them an edge in presentation because they remember the essential elements and the building blocks that structure the subject in a simple but profound way.

As adults age and acquire practical experience and more sophisticated knowledge on a subject, they are apt to present a subject skipping the essential elements and the developmental context needed for foundational steps in learning. This does not have to be. Nearly a decade after my mother passed at 92, I found one of her letters where she encouraged me to seriously consider my life and future. Mother wrote this short prayer at the end of her letter: *"Lord, give me the sense to see my faults, not all at once, but one by one, starting with my worst, then when I have that one under control to proceed to another. Lord, erase hostilities from me so that I may approach this day in peace, not to put my faith in people but in you."* Not a bad plan for a son to follow; at times we need to recall the lessons of parents, friends, and other caring folk whom God supplied to guide out journey.

Naturally, the words of mother had great impact on me. If she had faults I could not see, then I must be unaware of hidden faults in my own life. From the grave, the prayers of the past remain effective. Note in Luke 1:13 where the Messenger of the Lord told Zacharias, **"The prayer you no longer pray, God heard."** An elderly couple had stopped praying for a son, but God had already heard their prayer. The promised son was John, the Forerunner of Jesus. Perhaps we should have more confidence that God hears and will answers sincere prayers for the next generation. At times He may say "Yes, no or later," but He will hear and answer!

Dealing primarily with the basics should be enough to participate in the education of the young. Achievements, accomplishments and age do not have to hinder the sharing of information with others, provided it follows the K.I.S.S. formula: Keep It Short and Simple and includes the foundational steps that enabled the understanding of the subject at hand. Start at the learner's level of understanding and move the learner forward logically, step by step until learning becomes an exciting discovery of new and useful information.

Longevity and the age the subject matter was learned, or the experience occurred may factor into the process of sharing. As a Graduate Professor, it was difficult to teach young and inexperienced students who did not recall the introductory material or the elements essential to subject development. What was learned at 20 or 30 is difficult to teach at 50 or 60 to those without basic knowledge and the elemental steps which develop a subject. It appears as one matures, they begin to make assumption that basic facts are known, when this is not the case. Sadly, sharing subject matter becomes more sophisticated by the teacher and more complicated for the learner.

This is why each subject must start with a review of basic knowledge and developmental elements in order for the learner to grasp the scope and context of the subject in the curriculum. This difficulty can clearly be seen in new editions or volumes of a textbook.

For example, Earl Babbie in an early edition of *The Practice of Social Research*, provided details on how to develop an index for indirect surrogate measurement, but in the next edition simply wrote *"develop an index."* He was assuming the student knew the basic data as to how to assess facts which could not be directly measured. Why does this happen in textbooks? Publishers establish the size of a bookblock and when an author adds a paragraph or section to an existing textbook, an equal amount must be omitted to make room without adding to the number of pages in the text which influences the cover and the price. This complicates the learning process for students but manages to satisfy the self-worth of the author. The writer can show advance knowledge of the subject worthy of a new edition.

Those planning curriculum, course syllabi, and lesson plans or serious talks with the young, must consider that all sharing of subject matter must start with the basic elements of the subject and how this fits into life and structured curriculum. All learning must move from the known to the unknown. All knowledge is accumulative, incremental and progressive: *"precept upon precept, line upon line,"* (Isaiah 28:10-13} and at times the failure to learn a key fact may cause the engaging of content to crumble. A *precept* is a guiding principle or rule that is used to control, influence or regulate content and/or conduct. One may conceptualize a word, phrase or even a paragraph of subject matter without grasping the guiding principles or instructive elements intended as a directive for engaging the subject and grasping the broader implications and relevant functional application.

Good mentors, coaches and teachers are needed to keep the young on the straight and narrow way. My grandfather Green taught me many things of value. His guidance, joined with Mother's prayers, became fences on both sides of the road that kept me on the straight and narrow path. *God bless grandparents who truly care about their legacy investment in their children's children.*

Chapter 2

Complexity and Vagueness

Listening and learning stops when the complexity and vagueness of sophisticated or technical words are introduced without simplification. This is where an academic must become a scholar and use common sense and everyday words.

There is no all-embracing difference in the process of subject matter sharing whether for a book manuscript, a pulpit homily, a classroom lesson or a presentation of research findings in a lecture hall. The common concern is the informed participation of the audience. The objectives are clear; accurate and detailed sharing of specific subject matter. The intent and function of sharing data, information, or facts by speaker and location may be the only definable differences together with many similarities. There must be preparation, focus on the venue/audience, and comprehensive knowledge of the subject.

Complexity is a major obstacle to the transfer of subject matter by the helping professions. Normally, these professions are dealing only with the obvious needs of their clients. The social professions are confronted with an increasing volume of data relevant to both sacred and secular venues. Credentialed and gifted members of the helping professions are closer to the ultimate application of human knowledge-- life applications and have many opportunities to simplify and share their specialized knowledge with a captive audience or a cohort of students.

Human activities within the social professions are not always observable or easily separated into sacred, secular, or scholarly. Perhaps we should not even try to make a distinction: facts are facts regardless of their field of origin. All truth should be considered sacred, all defining and supported facts must be clearly stated and trustworthy, theories must never been considered settled law, and research findings must be reliable, trustworthy, and presented as a "snapshot" of a particular and limited sample in time and space and cannot be generalized beyond the population studied. Research must be replicated by others for validation.

While traveling by train from London to Birmingham, England in search of my English roots, many sheep were along the tracks, but there were no Shepherds in sight. Asking a fellow traveler if the Shepherds were on strike, the English lady declared, *"We do not have shepherds, Sir. We have fences."* My knowledge of sheep was limited to the Bible where Shepherds were prominent, but the lesson on the train taught me that human beings as sheep need both fences and shepherds. (Isaiah 53:6,7)

The sacred/secular dichotomy together with the academic/scholarly divide have over time with the added findings of researchers created differing perspectives on both life and subject matter. The complexity of human knowledge and the vagueness of spiritual life is beyond the comprehension of many. Culture and materialism together with the pleasures of life, blind many from developing a spiritual perspective of life and death. The whole truth is not that life is complicated but that it is sophisticated and requires an act of faith to accept the established reality so freely acknowledged by our ancestors and duly recorded in the sacred record. Without instinctive faith, a human being becomes a wandering jester trying to make sense of ambiguity without assurance of fairness in life and mercy in judgment.

Sometime ago a Hindu teenager asked, *"Why doesn't your religion teach reincarnation?* The answer was straight and forthright: *"Regeneration and reincarnation are cardinal tenants of the Christian Faith. Reincarnation is a **rebirth** and anyone who believes and follows Jesus becomes a new creation prepared for life and death. The issue of eternal destiny is actually settled while individuals are living, while some religions provide the faithful to receive a surprise at death's door."* Deciding the eternal destiny issue before death seems to be a clear-sighted and compassionate way to deal with the intuitive awareness of an extended afterlife.

Since God calls all levels of individuals to serve, it should be noted that some are called and qualifies without formal training for a role in situations where others would not venture. Long before the public education of children, or structured college training or seminary and advanced graduate study in higher learning were available, world leaders using honesty, common sense guidance from parents, practical training together with a work ethic and a transparency which made sense out of the uncertainty of life. As such people matured into leaders, they brought the world kicking and screaming out of intellectual, moral, or social darkness into a period of enlightenment and global progress.

A comparison of Luke and Paul, two well-educated men who together wrote one half of the New Testament, with Peter and John, noted as uncultured and uneducated men, would assist the understanding that different skills and knowledge are needed for different tasks.

> *When they saw the fearlessness and fluency of speech of Peter and John, and understood that they were uncultured and uneducated men, they were astonished; and recognized that they had been companions of Jesus. (Acts 4:13 EDNT)*

At least nine (9) of the first twelve Disciples were fishermen, who used their practical knowledge learned from daily work as a springboard for sharing the message of Grace. It is always good to remember that John, The Baptist, was a voice in the wilderness, wearing crudely woven garments made of camel's hair and ate migratory grasshoppers and wild honey. He preached a simple message of repentance to a listening crowd and announce the coming of Jesus. The following occurrence clearly speaks to this issue:

> A committee was charged with examining an individual for ministry in a homeless shelter. They were asked to consider him for "local preaching license." The candidate was asked to complete an extensive form for committee review. Members were amazed at the frankness and transparent honesty of this man. He came to faith late in life, what some would call a "late bloomer," and it was doubtful that his ministry would develop beyond the homeless shelter. His education was limited, and his natural gifts

were few, but he had a large dose of honesty, commonsense and was totally transparent with everyone. Exactly the kind of man the homeless men needed for this specific time in their lives. Sometimes he was confused by the questions, but mostly he was frank and open as he understood the questions.

On the question of sex, where he should have written "male" he wrote "2 or 3 times a week." To the question, "How long have you been preaching?" he answered, "Ain't been preaching, just exhorting." His most forthright and honest answer was to the question, "Have you been faithful to your wife since marriage?" The simple answer was, "No!" The committee assumed he spoke about his life before conversion, but no one on the committee had ever witnessed such transparent honesty and they asked no more questions.

> *"Love takes up where knowledge leaves off."*
> (Thomas Aquinas)

Since honesty is the best policy, and God does not call junk, the committee gave him an opportunity to do a "little exhorting" in the homeless shelter mission. He put his whole heart and soul into all his contacts with the men especially in each message at the mission. The men responded to his enthusiasm, unorthodox style and transparency. It is wonderful how God chooses and uses different folks with different strokes. The man for this place was a living example to the inner-city mission of what God could do when one totally surrenders to divine guidance Hopefully, God will provide a few more honest souls for life changing service to those who need a hand up not only a handout. Men and women who experienced a genuine relationship with Jesus and a transparent connection with souls on the byways of life who with an opportunity may become an asset to society.

Part of the difficulty in understanding clergy and teachers is their vocabulary. When a minister or a teacher deals with edification or instruction, there must be some simplification. The New Testament was written in the common language of the people and needed no explanation; it was the language of their childhood. In education, all students are taught to define words and/or specific terms at the first use or in a glossary of terms. A student begins with general competency: reading, writing, listening, speaking. As they move into more advanced subjects, they learn new terms and develop specialized competency. With the complexity of language, all unfamiliar words must be explained. The scourge of knowledge syndrome creates difficulty in the transfer of subject matter because some professionals are unable to adequately adjust their thinking and vocabulary to where the audience remains; consequently, little content is shared.

A Journal article, an academic thesis or a terminal degree dissertation always needs a glossary of specialized words and operational definitions for specific terms showing their contextual use in the manuscript. The reader or listener must clearly understand what the writer or speaker means by a word, phrase or the use of specialized jargon. Otherwise, the gobbledygook would complicate the understanding of the intended message. This is why the cultural, language, education and socio-economic status of an audience is important to a speaker. Also, relevant to sharing complex information is the fact: *"When one translates from another language and/or culture, the meaning changes."* Why? Because the meaning of words is in people, not dictionaries or the mind of learned academics.

Educators and ministers work in noble professions: *teachers* are considered **secular and neutral,** *clergymen* are judged to be **sacred and sectarian,** while *serious researchers* are normally accepted as **academic and scholarly.** Yet, behavior and performance are not apparent from fixed predispositions, viewpoints or the lifestyles of qualified individuals. Subject matter sharing may be classified by intention and delivery or generalized by location, subject matter or speaker, but the need for preparation and the principles and methods by which information is simplified and conveyed are directly related to the basic communication model. Although intention is the primary indicator that differentiate secular, sacred or scholarly communication, some individuals may attribute different forms of influence to various expositions or instruction. This is where prior knowledge, adequate preparation, the meaning of words, and informed participation enters the sharing and learning process.

Attempting to understand or explain the complexity and vagueness in the sacred, secular and scholarly fields requires simplification of the specialized words in the language involved. Authors and speakers may create differing perspectives on their focus, based on culture, personal education and language, but the complexity of human knowledge and the vagueness of new subject matter is beyond the comprehension of many. The basic facts of the subject are not complicated but are sophisticated and require simplification and clarification.

Early in constructing a graduate program for clergy who needed the knowledge and skill of social scientific research but were fearful of statistics because they viewed the process as mathematical. The solution: teach statistics as a language, a means to interpret and communicate facts and information. This worked well and developed social scientific researchers who made a worthy contribution to the sociological integration of religion and society.

From the Latin, **secular** has the meaning of *"worldly"* and **sacred** means *"holy."* In common usage, *secular* has a negative connotation for some and *sacred* may be used in a symbolic sense to show that something has value and is worthy of respect and should not be damaged or changed. However, sacred does not only mean "related to church or religion," and secular does not mean bad or unworthy. Normally, *secular* suggests a humanitarian and/or materialistic issue associated with business or the social sphere in the public square. *Sacred* is associated with things that are respected and honored by some and despised by others. The term **academic** ordinarily means a person who has studied under others and made certain scholarly achievement in a special field. **Scholarly** in this context has specific views and adopts specialized language into common words understood by the general population. Authors and speakers should utilize a basic concept of learning: that new facts are understood based on prior knowledge. The task is building a bridge from the "known to the unknown". (Gregory)

When a speaker disagrees with the facts, the meaning is often obfuscated. However, once the basics are clarified, comprehension begins. In sacred matters, it may take an act of faith as well as better definitions In the secular arena, technical or subject specific language must be broken into understandable parts and explained. In scholarly work the academic language must be studiously rendered into common words with the academic meaning expressed in simplified and clearly recognized words for an audience.

The classification of scholarly, secular and sacred may not be apparent from fixed attitudes and lifestyles of those who publicly share subject matter in various venues. However, the difference is blurred by culture, traditions and time. It appears the source of words is part of the problem without clear understanding of the tracked changes documented in unabridged resources there will be little transfer of data on a given subject.

Neutral and Secular: Teaching is presented as being *neutral* and as an educational function. Although the secular aspect of teaching suggests vocational, materialistic, and an association with social spheres and attempts to be neutral and impartial. Teachers normally are expected to present both sides of an issue and permit the learner to make up their own mind. This requires the control of personal bias. Even though, the general public considers the field of education to be neutral, academic disciplines develop a sense of importance until faculty assigned to a department often discriminate or develop a *"better than you"* bias with another discipline.

Often the jargon associated with a field of knowledge is seen by others to be judgmental and harsh. Specialized systems of research and style of documentation and research methods suggests they are superior to those of other disciplines. What can be done to advance general knowledge of known facts? Differences divide while commonalities advance unity, understanding and knowledge. Presenters and academic fields must seek commonalities to advance the sharing of specific information. *

> *Recommended: James Grier Miller's (1968) Living Systems Theory. Also see Chapter Four, Living Systems and Education, in Transformational Leadership in Education 2nd Ed. (2013) ISBN 978-1-935434-23-8, and/or Chapter Five, Living Systems and Research, in Designing Valid Research (2011) ISBN 9788-1-935434-57-3.

Disciplines are divided based on difference and must develop specialized terms and methods to achieve their assigned space in academia. Yet, the English faculty associate mathematicians only with numbers and as being weak in linguistics and overlooks their problem-solving abilities. The hard sciences look with pity on the soft sciences based on perceived methodological rigor, accuracy and objectivity. And some in the behavioral arena see little value in history and the social sciences. History students consider contemporary studies of global warming and social problems; such as, over-populated areas, famine and global political unrest as unnecessary energy and wasted funds. Therefore, a good teacher must work hard to maintain their valued status. This dilemma exists for clergy in different denominations contending with sectarian aspects of their training and daily and weekly function. *

> *An important concept initiated by Walter de Merton, founder of Merton College Oxford (1264) when he developed the statutes for an independent academic community included "a priest who serves the general public should not be trained by his own

order". Some see this construct as relevant to the broad public service required by present clergy.

Sectarian and Sacred: From an objective observer there is little difference in the expression of bias, intolerance, bigotry, partisanship, prejudiced and narrow-mindedness between those classified as secular or sacred based on their worldview. The divisions, known as sectarianism or denominations, in religion are similar to the divisions in education and higher learning which may be described by the same negative vocabulary. These facts may relate to the whole but not the parts. In each area there are clergy, teachers, and researchers who are doing their best to abide by an ethical code, academic honesty, moral living, and sharing truthful and useful subject matter with anyone who will listen, study and learn. However, it is difficult to be open-minded and forward-thinking and walk the "straight and narrow way".

The results are the same whether it is an immoral pastor, or a teacher without adequate concern and care for students, or an academic passing along fraudulent or flawed research findings that were funded by a company to deceive the public and support or damage a product currently on the market. There is a cancer growing on the sacred, the secular, and academic research aspects of subject matter sharing. Who is willing and able to remove the bad apples before they spoil the whole barrel? The case is not about the *idiom* of a *"the rotten apple in the barrel,"* but the idiots who cannot smell the bad apple or see the damage being done to others and take both punitive and preventive steps to clean up their system, whether sacred or secular.

It would be hard to refute the above if one reviewed a state university catalog or courses offered in faith-based educational institution and not see the same bias, partiality, one-sided teaching, intolerance for opposite points of view, and disrespect for anything or anyone who disagrees with their worldview. It would open the eyes of the public if exposure were available about those who were not abiding by the code of conduct to which they have ascribed loyalty by virtue of their present position of trust whether a pastor, professor or published author.

Academic and Scholarly: These two areas are well illustrated by Benjamin M. Spock, a Pediatrician who focused on the intellect and reason while others in pediatrics were concerned with the physical side of children. Knowing all the technological language of his medical discipline, Dr. Spock chose to write and speak in common language placing scholarly data about childcare in language that a teenage mother could understand and properly use. His core message was simple and profound. *"Don't be afraid to trust your own common sense. You know more than you think you do."* That is scholarship *par excellence*! The global public accepted his scholarship and purchased 50 million copies of his childcare book in his lifetime. Now, that is audience agreement and support. Many of us could learn a valued lesson from his approach to sharing specific information across roadblocks and boundaries which hinder learning. Academic and scholarly are classic higher educational endeavors for all writers and speakers that assist in removing complexity and vagueness in subject matter sharing.

A study of the science of interpretation *(hermeneutics)* and the art of speechmaking *(homiletics)* would be useful to anyone desiring to improve writing and speaking regardless of their field. The shared learning process is similar whether the data are shared by a credentialed clergyman, a qualified public-school teacher, or a scholarly academic researcher in a book or lecture. A lesson could also be taken from ancient historic documents preserved in world-class libraries.

The original text of historic documents preserved from the past were in appropriate language for the intended period and audience. No parsing, commentary or footnotes were necessary for their intended audience to understand. Perhaps the early writers never anticipated their work would be translated and somewhat mutilated by academics who did not fully understand their culture, people and time period. When the English academics transliterated the common Greek of the New Testament into the more academic language of Shakespeare, much of the original intent was lost for the reader. One can easily see what this did to the splintering of faith-based groups into sectarian divisions based on restricted and freeze-framed theology and name branded religion.

To get back to the original focus and find linguistics to express the authentic intent relative to a present-day audience is a demanding task. This necessitated long and boring study efforts to explain the tracked changes of words and at times exhausting lectures to make sense of what was intended to be a clearly understood message in the common language of the original audience. How many years of classic literature and language study does it take to comprehend cultural changes over time? What about those unable to take this academic journey? Who will simplify and extract the original intent of the ancient message from the present academic jargon?

Ancient rhetoric* clearly stated the need to establish not only *"what"* and *"why"* of speechmaking, but particularly *"who"* were the expected audience or readers. **What** was the purpose or the long-ranged direction of the message; **why** was the reason, either to inform, persuade or interpret the meaning to the specific and expected audience. All writers and speakers could benefit and improve the quality of sharing subject matter by following the rules of rhetoric and make application of the original intent of words. Otherwise they will be overcome by daily difficulties and sidetracked from the intended course of action and their audience will suffer great loss.

———*

> Just as in any written document, an early step is to determine the specific purpose or thesis for the composition. The thesis or purpose statement has three elements: **What, why**, and **who**. What are you writing about? Why are you writing (inform, persuade, or interpret)? And to whom are you writing. In the case of social research data is gathered from or about people or problems to describe, compare, or predict/explain their attitudes, knowledge, and/or behavior. . Social research that culminates in a published document must have a working title, a target population, and a central guiding reason or a **"why"**. In the case of social research data is gathered from or about people or problems to describe, compare, or predict/explain their attitudes, knowledge, and/or behavior. Social research that culminates in a dissertation must have a working title (what), a target population (who), and a central guiding reason to describe, compare, or predict/explain (why). In statistically supported research the hypothesis will have a measurement to test the relationship (**how**).

A college course on Advertising is remembered because the Professor was diligent in pointing out adds that deceived the public by imperfect or incomplete grammar. The assignment was to identify such adds. His example for the class were the tobacco companies who already knew of health hazards of smoking, supported fraudulent ads. *"More doctors smoke Camels than any other cigarette..."* according to English grammar, they cunningly suggested that knowledgeable medical doctors chose to smoke a particular brand of cigarettes. This was deceitful and endangered the health of a generation. What was incomplete in the grammar: *"than any other cigarette smokes Camels."* The class discovered many more, but the unsuspecting public is continually influenced by such ads.

The government used an unfamiliar word and declared tobacco to be *"carcinogenic,"* but the dictionary meaning was *"promoting the development of tooth decay."* **Great, smoking was just like candy!** It took 50 years (1964-2014) for Congress to see the light on the end of a cigarette as harmful to public health. It took much political will to get past the lobbyists and simply declare *"tobacco products may cause cancer."* Finally, when smoking began to impact the Military budget and the cost of health care and insurance, the labeling of tobacco products became more realistic. Congress remained under the influence of lobbyists who worked for the tobacco companies. There are many unintended consequences of regulations and falsely named legislation passed by Congress.*

*My younger sister sat between two smokers on an airplane who were told she was extremely allergic to tobacco; yet, they exercised their rights and smoked anyway. She went into a coma with drastic results. I testified twice before a subcommittee of Congress relative to the hazards of smoking in confined spaces particularly on airplanes, but it took decades to make significant changes in attitudes and actions.

In this context, integration is to make whole or new by adding or bringing together parts. Positive social change and cultural integration takes place at the level of ideology and identity produced by philosophy and theology. These in turn create values, ideas and social roles. A study of the processes governing thought and conduct including *aesthetics, ethics, logic, metaphysics, morals, character and behavior* is known as **Philosophy**. On the other hand, **Theology** is a study of interaction between a Higher Power and the universe as to *moral matters, relationship integrity and transparent behavior*. The study of theology and philosophy creates *Ideology* and *Identity*; from the combination of these one develops value and ideas and the system of social roles.

At the levels of ideology and identity, different individuals and divergent groups find common ground to shape positive social change and influence integration aspects in society. **Ideology** is formation in the affective domain where ideas of an individual or class are derived exclusively through feelings. All aspects of integration take place at the level of ideas and values. Nevertheless, to develop an **Identity** and meaningful ideas and worthy values one must have an elementary understanding of the integration of theology and philosophy.

Comparing key aspects, one could clearly see meaning and value in the role of pastor, public speaker,

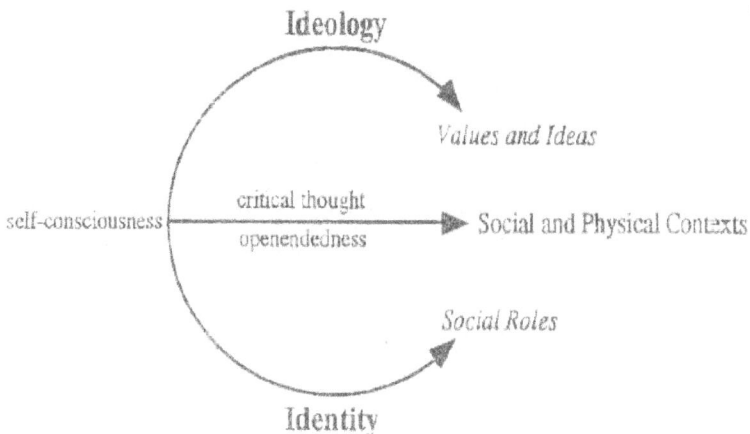

classroom teacher and academics doing social scientific research and reporting findings: they are, best described as having *"a hands on approach to a nurturing profession with service to others through skill and occupational craft for speaking and working with people that produce positive social change."*

Below are short definitions of essential elements in the social professions from which the above process was generalized. Social or helping professions are identified and sustained by these constructs:

Assisting — *nurturing well-being as a life coach*

Calling — *a special direction in life*

Career — *forward moving with specific guidance*

Craft — *hands on approach to positive development*

Commitment — *mature attitude toward social change*

Passion — *excitement for knowing and sharing*

Service — *unselfish service directed toward others*

Vocation — *use of occupational crafts and skills*

The objective of the social professions includes the sharing of beneficial ideas and values to assist those they serve. To share workable ideas and demonstrate worthy values, authors and speakers of all stripes and sophistication would profit by reading in the field of philosophy. It is not by accident that the community of scholars identifies the highest educational achievement as a PhD or Doctor of Philosophy. In the same manner, the clergy and leadership related to religion, covet the graduate identity ThD or Doctor of Theology. Why, because these academic identities provide confidence and assurance that the subject matter being shared is studied and sourced from authenticated documents and taught by learned teachers who perhaps emulate Paul, the best educated writer of the New Testament.

2. And entrust the things you learned from me which were confirmed by many witnesses, to faithful men who will be competent to teach others also. (2 Timothy 2:1-2 EDNT)

The information they use to construct their purpose-directed thought systems is often the product of higher education to which an audience or classroom are not prepared to receive without simplification and direct application. The training of most qualified professionals has not given adequate attention to the preparation and delivery process of sharing relevant subject matter with their clientele.

An old German professor of Medieval History in a public university taught me more early church history and facts about two principal characters of the Book of Acts that were never mentioned later in seminary. One day as he lectured about the influence of cities on the historic development of organized religion, he stopped abruptly and mused softly, *"Was that Paul's second or third missionary journey? He further deliberated, "The first half of Acts was about Peter and the last half was about Paul."* Then a spark of cognition provided data on a city crucial to his lecture and he continued. This was a class sidebar that demonstrated the professor's thinking and gave the class insights from his years of study that were beneficial to those interested in history and religion.

Higher education and professional credentialing are concerned with consistent thinking and observation in the content of a field of knowledge. They may not be adequately prepared for close and personal encounters serving others with *off script facts of value*. Systems of thought persons who are provided with the same information to arrive at similar conclusions. Likewise, methods of observation have been devised to ensure that observers can record a particular observation in a manner that recognizes it as beneficial guidance.

Such public thought and observations are fundamental to the specialized function of a minister, classroom teacher or academic researcher dealing with methods to discover answers to questions relative to the solution of problems. However, the social professions have opportunity to share facts that could broaden the learning process for those in their care. Rules and restrictions may cause the sharing of facts without adequate application; consequently, needed guidance is lost.

Authors and speakers must structure a paradigm shift from the standard procedures for transferring information to innovative ways often neglected by current systems. This would assist listening and enable learning in innovative and practical ways often neglected in the educational and professional systems and would reduce complexity and vagueness through scholarly simplification.

(Rendering of Job 14:1-2 EDOT)

Troubled days follow human birth;
As a suckling reaches Mother earth.
A stumbling earthling emerges to life;
Bursting forth with a budding delight.
Walking with a stumbling gait;
Trouble lurks at the garden gate.
Youth blossoms in the morning light;
Withering age is reaped before night.
The frailty of life takes a final nod;
Reaching for the hand of a loving God.

Chapter 3

Direction and Guidance

*The personal roles and professions
which deal directly with people
and their needs are the
substance, structure and strength
of human development.*

Direction once with guidance often: this is what human beings must understand about the purpose and direction of their professional journey. When NASA pointed a rocket in the direction of the moon, it had included in the complex structure of the space craft a sophisticated guidance system. This was a build-in system for the eventuality the rocket would get off course. Should the rocket deviate slightly from the programed course, the guidance mechanism would function much as the autonomic nervous system of the human body: it would act spontaneously and do whatever was necessary to put the rocket back on course. There was an established directional course and a guidance system in place for constant use should the craft venture off course. Direction once with guidance often: this is what human beings must understand about the purpose and direction of their professional journey. Early training, educational preparation, specific direction and specialized guidance are needed to reach the desired objective.

Primarily what was learned about a career path came from family, friends and common sense. My mother was a teacher and took great pains to guide my early educational growth, but when my career turned toward faith-based service, the ministry and teaching, she had second thoughts. Why? Because at times those in one profession may not clearly understand the process that pulls one to another profession. Yet, understanding that my intention was primarily ministry through education, the commonality became clear: teaching and ministering were two helping professions concerned with positive growth and development in others. When the obvious objective of positive social change for individuals, families, local communities and society became clear mother was supportive.

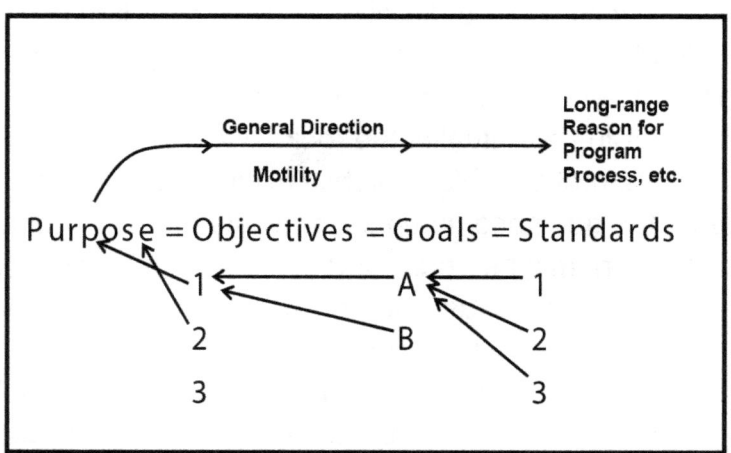

A purpose is the general direction or long-range reason for action. Although, "intention" may include *purpose, objectives, goals, and standards for evaluation.* The *desired outcome* or purpose points toward a general direction while *intention* includes a guiding predisposition which operates long-term to accomplish an objective which is a sub-set of the purpose. This leads to intermediate goals which are evaluated by common standards or criteria.

Perhaps directional guidance gets back to *"intention"* rather than dealing with *"function"* which is the *proper or particular way of operation* would clarify matters. Understanding or feeling the pull of a directional purpose may be that which pushes one toward a particular lifestyle or profession, while intentionality provides a deep-seated guidance mechanism along the journey. Consequently, sacred and secular may no longer be relevant to the function of basic communication in subject matter sharing regardless of the purpose, speaker or location. Relevance may well depend on the scholarly handling of subject matter with total consideration of the audience. How will the audience hear, understand, and apply the subject matter presented? The basic principles of personal communication are generic and are applied equally to all forms of writing and speaking.

The direction toward a social profession should start early in life. All who desire to assist others will need specific direction and special guidance. Normally, vocational direction is provided once, but along the professional journey guidance is available to prevent a catastrophe. Just as a rocket pointed to the moon has a designated direction, it also has a logical guidance system to keep it on track during the long voyage. When one starts a career path to a social profession, guidance from many sources will be needed to stay on course. This guidance comes in many forms: a parent, a dedicated teacher, a book, a prayer, a spiritual leader, a system of rules, and of course the formal instruction in a course of study provided a predisposition to learn exists and functions within rules and expectations of others.

The social professions require more than an education. One needs the pull of a calling, a career path, a concern for others, the dexterity of a craft, and a passion for growth and development. Basic experience working with people and learning about the practical side of life and work create a foundation for a profession. One must be thoroughly prepared for a social profession in order to assist and nurture others at great personal cost and even material sacrifice. Never disregard practical experience and a deep love for people.

The helping professions are more than a vocation, they become a way to serve others and participate in positive social change within families, communities, and in the common aspects of society. The personal roles and professions which deal directly the needs of people are the substance, structure and strength of human development. They provide both direction and guidance toward change and build fences, write rules of engagement, and shepherd individuals through the process. At times, professionals are surprised at people God uses to declare His Truth in a particular situation.

Attending college classes in West Virginia, a tent preacher came to town. Some of the students went out of curiosity and were surprised that an uneducated man could confuse scripture and still teach valuable lessons. Obviously, the old preacher could not read, so his wife would read scripture on which he gave commentary in his "so called" sermon. The first night the wife read from Galatians 6:1, *"Oh, thou foolish Galatians, who has '***be-switched***' you."* The actual word was "bewitched," but he took a cue from her mistake and declared, *"Don't let the devil switch you on a sidetrack."* He spoke of the main railway line and the spur tracks that led to the coal mines. He warned the audience to stay on the mainline and that the sidetrack just goes to a hole in the ground. It was a simple message which communicated a valuable lesson to a crowd of coal miners (and probing college students).

The next night his wife read from Jude 1:4 about people who *"creep in unaware"* so he picked up on her reading and said, *"Some people try to creep in under the wire without repenting of their sins."* He pontificated about people joining a church without conversion and some seeking water baptism without repentance and said, *"I don't care if you are baptized until every fish in the river knows you by name, that won't save you without repentance!"*

The other messages were equally revealing. He shared from Deuteronomy 28, that it was better to be the *"Head and not the Tail"* and spoke of keeping up and not lagging behind. March at the head of the parade, don't bring up the rear! *"Don't let the Lord lay you off"* was another message sent straight to the coal miners. He declared, *"Essential workers are never laid off."* He challenged the miners to be effective workers and to be active in witnessing. He didn't say it exactly in those words, but the words he used communicated with the attentive audience who was listening and learning.

The old preacher told us that God even used a donkey, he said *"a Jack Ass!"* when the prophet would not carry the true message. He reminded the people that even *"the rocks and the trees would cry out"* if the truth were not declared. God can use anyone willing to share

His message. Those required to share spiritual truth, were needed to reach a broader audience. An honest heart with good intentions were sufficient to witness and share the message of grace, but it depends on the audience to whom God sends the messenger. In addition to a divine call, education assists in the preparation of material, but the public speaking must be divinely guided to be effective. Perhaps we should trust God to send more plain-spoken individuals who will not flinch from declaring what they believe to be the whole counsel of God.

Contacts and Context Create Needs

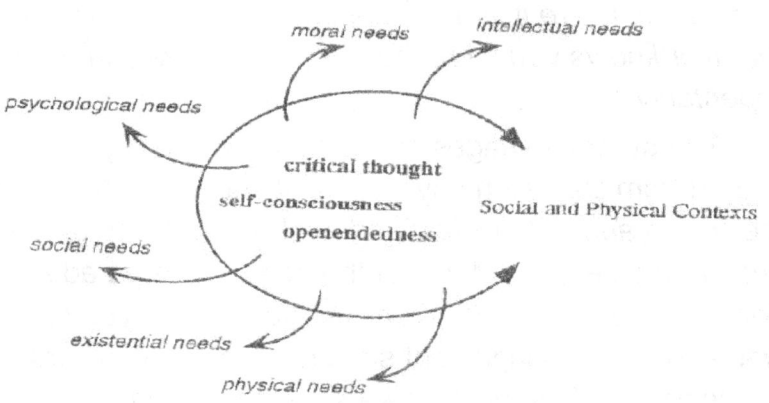

Notwithstanding, their cultural background, ethnicity, language, or education, human beings share basic qualities: *self-consciousness, critical thought, and open-endedness.* The interaction of these qualities with the physical and social contexts of relationships create certain needs. These needs are *physical, existential, social, moral, psychological and intellectual.* unselfish service to others, is not determined by education, social status or how one earns a living, but by a sincere connection with Higher Authority and a mature connection with others. When behavior is connected with vocation or influenced by money, the proper function of a calling becomes unclear and often undefinable. The love of money always dilutes and weakens the positive sharing of gifts and developed talents. There is an old story about a pastor of a small rural congregation who received a call to a more affluent city church. The report was that a deacon confronted the pastor that he was leaving just because the other place had more money. The old pastor replied, *"True brother, more money means there is more wickedness there and those good folks need me more because they are in the midst of city-wide wickedness."*

7. For we brought nothing into this world, neither can we carry out anything. 8. Let us be content with food and clothing. 9. But those who are determined to be rich are tempted and caught in a trap, and into many senseless and dangerous appetites, such desires cause men to sink into present destruction and later punishment in hell. 10. <u>For the root of all evil is the love of money: while some craving money have wandered away from the faith and suffered many self-inflicted and discouraging sorrows.</u> *11. It is for you, servant of God, to run from these things; and pursue righteousness, godliness, faith, love, endurance, and be teachable. 12. Struggle to win the good fight of faith and grasp eternal life, to which you were called, now that you have witnesses to your noble profession.* (1 Timothy 6;7-12 EDNT)

After a chapel speech at a Kentucky College, an elderly teacher approached who was the Professor of

English Grammar. My question was *"How many dangling participles did I have?"* Her answer, *"Just two, but you communicated well with the students."* It was most encouraging that formal education was improving my public speaking. Learning from a Professor of English Grammar who listened attentively to my speech, she answered my question. It stifled my speaking a few times, especially being conscious that some listen intently to catch even small grammatical mistakes that distract from the intended message. In college it was the teacher's red ink, in publishing it is an editor's blue pencil, and in speaking it is the *"yellow light"* of the listener. These all caution speakers to use Standard English grammar with a mature and educated audience.

Some years ago, Southern Baptist identified the 400 fastest growing churches in their convention. As a member of the Fellowship of SBC Researchers, my observation that a majority of these churches were led by bi-vocational pastors was informative. Pastors supported themselves and their families by continued involvement in a career that predated their entry into ministry. Also, during this time acquired data disclosed that men who dropped out of a pastorate actually returned to their previous work. The loss of capable manpower needed to advance a local congregation was a lesson lost in the celebration of numerical growth. Could this possibly explain SBC's losses in baptisms and new members during the next decades? Somehow leadership forgot that life moves forward looking in a rear-view mirror. The future is always influenced by the past.

What was surprising was that most pastors previously worked in people-related areas of the economy: sales, marketing, or endeavors such as teaching and insurance which had a beneficial effect on the family. Some speculated that had they properly used their prior knowledge and previous work experience to guide and enhance their ministry, they may have continued in their calling. God does not call junk and those with a call are prepared and equipped for their work but must *"endure hardship as a good soldier."* There is no discharge in the battle against evil and the struggle to make disciples. Those called must preserver in their work using every ounce of practical and previous work-related experience in the fulfillment of their worthy career. They must bloom where God plants.

The Garden edict: *earn bread by your sweat all your days*, made the "sweat cloth" a symbol of hard work. Luke (19:20-28) shared a story where Jesus expressed grave concern for a man who was furnished resources but did not use them properly (Genesis 3:19). This idle servant wrapped the gift in his "sweat cloth" for safe keeping, because he did not intend to work, but just wait for his master to return. This did not please Jesus!

>Data about the "sweat cloth, napkin, or handkerchief" was found in an early papyrus marriage contract as part of the dowry. Since the cloth was for a working man, the father of the bride would pass to the new husband a "sweat cloth" signifying *"I have worked and supported this my daughter from birth until now; that responsibility is now on your shoulders."* The clear message *"Go to work and support my daughter and her children; they are a part of my extended family and essential to my legacy."* A true legacy cannot be established without hard work... cooperation and a "sweat cloth" will be needed!

When a group of Disciples were together after the Death of Jesus, Peter was discouraged and decided to return to his former fishing business. He said to the others, who were mostly former fishermen, *"I am going fishing.* They said, *"We will go with you."* They went out immediately and got into a boat; and that night they caught nothing."* This was a return to their previous work because they were experienced fishermen. (John 21:1-14). It was after this that Jesus instructed Peter to return to his new task and *"feed My lambs and My sheep."*

It was time for specific guidance and transitional growth from using only fishing know-how to use additional knowledge gained by learning all that *"Jesus began to do and teach."* Shepherding sheep was a common vocational task of which most adults were aware. It was practical knowledge not being used that could encourage the transition to new leadership. Not only fishing know-how, but the addition of practical knowledge of care and feeding of sheep was to become part of their service to followers. First they were to *"catch men alive"* for kingdom work. Now, they must add the shepherding of young and growing disciples. Jesus said, *"feed My sheep."* This was the process of enabling converts and followers to *"grow in grace and knowledge"* and a way to strengthen and support the learners.

During their time with Jesus, they learned more about expectations of their calling and the danger of losing focus. Jesus previously said,

> *Simon, Simon, watch out, Satan has desired to have you that he may sift you as wheat: 32. But I have prayed for you, that your faith fail not: and when you return to Me,* **strengthen your brethren.** *(Luke 22:31-32)*

When the fishermen were called to follow Jesus, they were told that Jesus would teach them to use their fishing know-how to *"catch men alive"* for kingdom work. This meant that Peter and the other fishermen were now to utilize their extended practical and common knowledge of shepherding to care for and equip those previously gathered as followers of the Way. With Peter's renewed leadership and the assistance of the other fishermen, the work of equipping learners to become messengers to advance a message of good will to all could proceed with haste. Jesus had clearly taught *"As the Father sent me, so send I you!"* The contract had been sub-let to the newly formed team.

Peter had overlooked a personal message left in the Garden Tomb. When John and Peter ran to the Garden, they found the grave clothes of Jesus that had been hardened with oil and spices still in the form of a man, but the napkin or *"sweat cloth"* that covered the open place at the face was removed, folded neatly and laid aside. Why? So Peter could see into the grave clothes and know the Jesus had been raised. The *"sweat cloth"* as a recognized symbol of hard work was *"folded and placed separately"* to send a strong message to Peter. *"As the Father sent me, so send I you! I have finished my work and will return to My Father. It is now your time to take up the task and do the labor to advance the Kingdom."* The task of reaching the sharing what they had learned to make new disciples had been sub-let to Peter, the Apostles, and to all who followed Jesus. That was expressed in the general Challenge of Jesus after the Resurrection. (Matthew 28:19,20)

Faith-based leadership is often influenced by early work experience in their service to others. Perhaps this is why God calls different folks with different strokes for different posts of service. Some years ago, an awareness of such cases came to my attention:

- An expert Bible salesman developed such familiarity with the product he was selling, that he became an excellent bible teacher and preacher.

- An electric vacuum cleaner salesman who was able to convince rural folk without electricity that power was coming and they needed his product to properly clean their homes. He would share: "The telephone pole is just about a mile down the road and they are moving this way....you need an electric vacuum cleaner, to better clean your home." This early work experience brought to life his ability to persuade people living in moral darkness to permit the light to shine on a way to clean up their life and gain new hope for a better future. His work experience was translated into subject matter sharing.

- A postman carrying letters to all kinds of people was impressed by the unofficial motto of the postal service, "Neither snow nor rain nor heat nor gloom of night stays these couriers from the swift completion of their appointed rounds." This caused the postman to begin the bi-vocational work of an evangelist by carrying letters written by, Mark, Luke, John, James, Paul ,et al with a God's stamp of approval for personal delivery to the housebound souls and unchurched along his postal route.

The social professions are normally rooted in morality and a sound upbringing that comes from home environment and early educational guidance. Those who serve should never abandon those strengths and motives that push and pull one toward helping others. This reasoning is based in an early developed work ethic that provided basic skills and the wisdom to accept others as they are and serve their needs. Early work experience provides the basic tools needed to adequately serve others. It is assumed that acts of kind-heartedness in lifestyle is a positive avenue for personal and social change. This enables a better understand of the scriptural injunction *"Abide in the calling wherein you are called."* (1 Corinthians 7:20, 24)

During World War II, Dr. A. E. Wilder-Smith, a Swiss Pharmacologist, took his family to England for safety. Because he was bilingual with a medical and military background, the British asked that he become Supervisor of a Luftwaffe Prison Camp for German airmen. He accepted the difficult task and experienced unusual cooperation from the German prisoners until they thought their food rations were being cut in half.

One morning when the Germans arrived for breakfast, they saw half loaves of bread on the table. The top-ranking German protested to Dr. Wilder-Smith about the cut in rations. The simple explanation showed an increase in rations was a transforming experience. It seems that the women of a nearby village, in an act of humanitarian kindness, decided to share their bread ration with the prison camp. The women brought half-loaves of bread to the prison. This act of human kindness so shocked the German psychic that most of the hardline German airmen had a drastic change of heart, developed a new mindset, and professed this moral, ethical, and spiritual change to Dr. Wilder-Smith. It is the only recorded event of exponential positive social change in a single population during the war years.

As a result, Dr. Wilder-Smith perhaps misread his role and began to consider his influence in this positive social change as future guidance for his career. After the war, he chose not to return to medicine, his original sphere of influence, but to become somewhat of a spiritual advocate for change sharing good news and working with college students in Europe. He had some success in changing a few lives but was unable to reach anyone connected to the medical profession. He became discouraged and returned to his previous career and immediately became a force for change in the lives of medical students, interns, and medical professionals. What was the difference? He had returned to the strength and experience of his original calling—the Medical Profession. He had ventured a little off the previous path of his life, probably because of the stressful changes caused by the destruction of war.

Why Does God Allow it? It was my privilege to hear Dr Wilder-Smith speak about this part of his life in Chicago at the announcement of his book, *Why Does God Allow it? — why do bad things happen to good people?* His speech made clear to me the words of Paul *"Let each one remain in the calling wherein he was called."* And again *"Let each man abide with God where he is called"* (1 Corinthians 7:20, 24 EDNT). The Knox (1945) version makes the concept even clearer:

> *"Everyone has his own vocation, to which he has been called; let him keep to it."* And further *"Each of you is to remain, in the condition in which he was called"* (1 Corinthians 7:20, 24 Knox).

Finally, note the wise saying, **"Bloom where God plants you!"**

As adults age and gain practical experience and more sophisticated knowledge on a subject, they are apt to present the subject skipping the essential elements and the developmental context needed for foundational learning. Mature adults must include the essential elements and building blocks that structure the subject in a simple way. The age the subject matter was learned, or the experience occurred factors into the process of sharing. As adults matures, many make the false assumption that the basic facts are known, when this is not the case. Mature teachers may have difficulty teaching complicated data to young and inexperienced students because they do not recall the introductory material or the elements essential of subject development.

 A young pilot who was privileged to fly a gifted engineer up the Amazon River in search of a suitable place to construct a dam, asked *"Sir, since you are a well-educated and experienced man, do you have any rules for progress?"* The engineer responded, *"I have three rules for progress.* **The first one is, never give up what you have gained.***"* The engineer returned to observation of the river and the pilot concentrated on his flying. Sometime later the pilot asked, *"What are the other two rules?"* The answer *"They have not been written, if you keep the first one you need no other rules."* Provided the old engineer was correct, all that is needed to become effective in a career is to *"never give up what has been learned from parents, books, teachers and early work experience."* This becomes a way to abide in your lifetime calling. The execution of that calling may be tweaked as conditions change, but the essential direction and intent remain.

 It is obvious that many New Testament personalities were identified by their work experience. Since faith-based vocations in the early days were not salaried positions as they are today, the basic and foundational guideline of *"abiding in a vocational calling"* were clearly related to their economic and work-based qualification. Although well-educated Paul was a known *"tentmaker."* The craft of tentmaking was learned from Israel's earliest days of semi-nomadic existence in the time of the patriarchs. This trade carried over into the life and work. Paul, Aquila, and Priscilla all made their living by making tents (Acts 18:3). Luke was identified as a *"medical"* person. Obviously both Paul and Luke used their prior training, experience and knowledge as a support factor in their continued faith-based work. Their work experience was a foundation for their physical and dedicated service to others. In fact, according to a wise man *"Everything you do prepares you for everything you do!"*

Consequently, a clergyman, a teacher, a political statesman, a scientist, a doctor, a lawyer, merchant or thief may be drawn toward a special way of life by a sense of destiny or some predetermined life course. Not only public service, but many feel the pull or drive of a "calling" or "mission" to participate with a passion in a particular vocation or profession. Since calling is *"a strong urge toward a particular way of life, career, or vocation"* individuals other than speakers and teachers may feel an urge or pull toward a particular career or way of life depending on their character, family, education, socio-economic status, environment, and/or opportunity. This is part of the divine direction for each life.

Most of the original disciples were fishermen, who later used their fishing know-how to *"catch men alive"* for kingdom work. Paul's tentmaking skill provided financial support for him and his traveling crew. He also used his knowledge of construction and the functional assistance for others to guide his thinking about gathering learners for advancement. Luke's medical training and experience caused him to write about the functional behavior of Jesus by gathering *"all that Jesus began to do and teach."* In a story only in Luke's Gospel he identified the medical function of a stranger better known as the Good Samaritan. And in the Acts, Luke chronicled the functionality and continuing development of leaders by comparing and contrasting Peter and Paul. The first half of Acts was about Peter and the last half about Paul. His understanding of human behavior and his medical experience is obvious in the vocabulary used in both Luke and Acts. A primary lesson: *early work experience informs later service to others.*

One thing a fisherman learned in the early days was to mend their nets and prepare the boat for the next day. This speaks to a second-mile approach to life (taking the long view). Under Roman Law, a soldier could compel a stranger to carry his load for one mile further in the direction they were traveling. When Jesus was asked about obedience of this regulation, His response, *"If you are compeled to go one mile, go the second mile of your own accord."* All faith-based action requires a "second-mile" attitude. My Grandfather put it this way: *"Do more than is required and you will always have a job."* When one becomes aware that *"the end is worth the struggle of the journey,"* they normally are encouraged to move ahead guided by family, friends and the rules of engagement. This is the benefit of the long view in life and work.

Knowhow became guidelines for future service. Jesus saw Peter's experience as a fisherman as a carryover into discipleship; therefore, Jesus told Peter, *"I will make you a fisher of men (teach you to catch men)."* Jesus used a word meaning *"to catch alive"* used only twice in the New Testament. Peter was to use his fishing know-how as guidelines for catching men alive and useful for kingdom work. Just as a dead fish had little value, a follower without a willingness to work was worthless. Later, Paul declared, *"We instructed you that if any would not work, neither should they eat"* (2 Thessalonians 3:10). The work ethic established in the Garden of Eden has not been rescinded but has been extended for the duration of life of all who populate Mother Earth, even those whom God uses to continue His mission.

> *...pursue righteousness, faith, love, peace with the ones calling on the Lord out of a clean heart. 23. But foolish and ignorant questions avoid, knowing they breed nothing but arguments. 24. And the servant of the Lord must not struggle with arguments; but behave kindly toward all men, teaching appropriately with unwearied tolerance, 25. understanding those who oppose in order to instruct properly; if perhaps God will change their mind to acknowledge the truth; 26. having been captured by the will of God they may remove themselves from the trap of the devil. (2 Timothy 2:22-26 EDNT)*

Chapter 4

Listening and Learning

Social communication is about introductory steps that lead to useful information related to family, career, and a positive future.

Listening is a high form of human contact close to actually physically touching a person. The early nature of the teaching/learning process was normally based on the sharing of information. Active learning is introduced when data information, and facts begin to form an undeveloped mixing bowl for storage in a long-term memory bank. Most future learning is based on facts in this memory reserve provided there is a developed capacity for recall. A better system had to be found for comprehensive learning and for mature students with life-long responsibilities.

Early learning enables the active student to adequately process information with the intention of answering questions and/or solving problems. When questions are answered and problems are solved, new knowledge is formulated and stored in the long-term memory bank. This is the actionable knowledge used in future encounters with family life and career.

Presentation of the message content and the listening-learning process is fact-based. Whether the words are from a pulpit, the report of research findings in a lecture hall or the instruction in a classroom, all employ the basic elements of social communication which relate to the transfer of subject matter from sender to a receiving audience. The presenter, the venue, the inattentive audience all create noise. A failure to listen with the intent to learn becomes part of the noise that hinders positive learning which creates a failure of analysis and action and adequate dialogue responses to subject matter sharing.

Sharing of subject matter is often in problematic venues or in sensitive situations which create static or noise that hinder the receiver. Where a presenter must compete with the static of distractions or the non-verbal noise of an inattentive audience, more care must be given to basic communications. Without disciplined listening there will be no acquisition of useful information which may eventually be stored in the long-term memory.

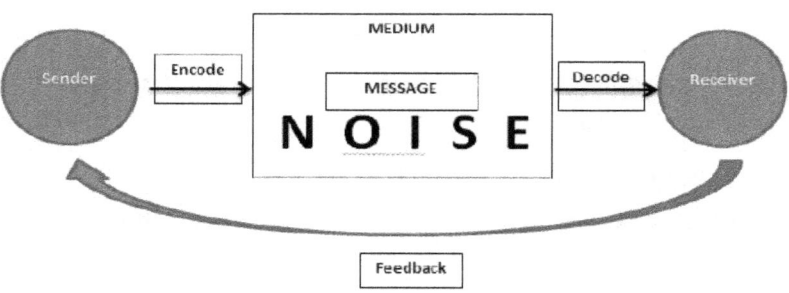

Consider the three levels of hearing: (1) level of non-hearing or being oblivious to the subject at hand; (2) the level of hearing words without meaning (even notetaking of those words without understanding); and (3) level of active listening, which requires analysis and action. Unless a listener is at level three there will be little if any actual learning of shared subject matter.

A possible answer to the required encoding and decoding may be hidden in Shakespeare's prose, *"a rose by any other name would smell as sweet."* The full meaning of the "rose" example is lost in the vagueness of past culture and language. In past literature, the rose has indicated passion and promise, an obvious balance which conveyed a new beginning or a rosy future. However, in the sharing/learning process the "rose" could easily represent the pleasant fragrance of listening and learning. The blessing of sharing useful information with learners has great value for both the learner and teacher. The years of disciplined study has come to fruition in sharing and receiving process.

A deeper appreciation for learning would occur f all involved understood that data, information and/or facts are not knowledge *in isolation*; they are simply a means to an end and must be used to answer a question or solve a problem to become usable knowledge by others. This means the listener must engage the shared material and embrace the part that stimulates understanding and growth in a positive direction. Analysis and action are required to turn listening into a significant learning experience.

A half century ago professionals saw communication as a one-way process. Authors and speakers assumed that what was written or spoken was received unbroken and fully understood. With practical experience and research in the nature and function of basic communications, professionals began to recognize that individuals and audiences were different and subject matter sharing had to be placed in the context of the listener. Also learned over time was that context of the listener or an audience was situational and dynamic. The concept and character of two-way communication was enhanced by the early concern and research of Kurt Lewin, et.al. in the field of positive social change.

To engage the mind to analyze and act on what is heard does not come easily. First, there is an audience *"with ears but hears nothing,"* because they are daydreaming or unprepared to listen. Second, there is hearing which receives words without understating and may even be able to repeat the terms and language without comprehending their value or significance. Finally, there is the level of listening which clearly requires a situational analysis of content and purposeful action to utilize what was learned. Such analysis and action constitute a substantial learning experience because the mind is engaged to listen and learn.

All present and future knowledge is built on the past foundation stones and the uncomfortable footsteps of early academics or the breaking of new ground by pioneers. In reality, almost everything done by the human race is influenced directly by the past, their present survival and upward mobility for career and family. It was assumed that unveiling the process of sharing subject matter regardless of the person or place would be similar to opening an historic buried time capsule containing data on religion, the human race, and practical learning from experience and education.

Perhaps the cache of information was intended to communicate to a future audience something about the past that would provide better understanding of the history of a people, their time, work, lifestyle behavior and gained knowledge. Whether we profit from this gift of knowledge as an inheritance depends on building on the foundation of past learning and gaining more to leave a legacy for future generations. Without listening and learning there will be no legacy.

Learning in theory is both intellectual and rational. The difference in learning is primarily source of instruction. The teacher must excite and direct the self-activity of the learner and get them involved. In reality, the educational process is a highly emotional and interpersonal practice and requires a combination of intellectual excitement and interpersonal rapport. There must be an empathy relationship between teacher and learner. This is a trust relationship with firm reliance on the integrity and ability of the teacher and a concern for learning expressed by the student. The faculty directed learning model works only with integrity and trust.

A sanctuary homily and classroom lesson normally have a passive audience, while group discussion generally creates more involvement in the subject at hand. New and fresh material and research findings create a better understanding and feedback. The weakness of most public speaking is increased without feedback correction because the basic elements of communications are unsatisfied. Even non-verbal feedback is important to the speaker.

In an early pastorate while still working on my education, there were several retired clergy in membership. One in particular, R. P. Johnson, was an experienced leader and pioneer preacher in whom many had great confidence. In my Monday morning coffee sessions at his home, questions were asked and evaluation made about my speaking. One Monday he said, *"You seem to make an effort in each message to present something that no one has ever thought of or seen in scripture before."*

> [As a young pastor searching for the original intent of koine Greek words and attempting to render this meaning into a common English expression, while making a relevant application, his observation surprised me.]

"When God gives you a new message, you can use it again anytime the same need is present. The same way the Choir or Soloist repeats a good song."

> [I did not understand but accepted his constructive criticism. My effort was to understand the written word and present what was learned creatively in the time allotted.]

With the development of more maturity and speaking experience, his words were recalled and the *"recycled homily"* ideas began to be useful. However, when the ideas were used again, they were warmed over with earnest meditation and fresh study using a new "key word" and a different "interrogative" to structure a new approach to the same content material. Covering old ground without a fresh perspective would be boring and the audience would most certainly receive the non-verbal message. Such feelings cannot be hidden, grinning like a Cheshire cat will not cover the disappointment of plowing through old material. New subjects, new material, and new ways of delivery are important to the speaker's presentation.

Without a fresh message there will be a loss and the listeners would sense this loss. The audience will usually model the attitude of the speaker.

After speaking in St. Croix, USVI, on "Intercessory Prayer" a young girl, new to Protestant worship, wrote me a note: *"I enjoyed your speaking, I like stories about people's lives. I enjoyed Mrs. Green's singing, it was warm, soft, and comfortable."* Then to show she clearly understood my message, she wrote: **"And prayer is just like jam, you can't spread even a little without getting some on yourself."** Consider the meaning of (Matthew 18:3): *Except you are converted and become as a child, you shall not enter the Kingdom of heaven.* If the children do not understand, their parents and other adults will never comprehend the message or make a practical application of truth to life.

Another incident occurred in Arkansas confirmed that a young and open mind will receive the content of a properly prepared and presented message. A young girl who normally was in Children's Church on Sunday and stayed with a baby-sitter during all evening services, came to my Sunday through Wednesday services because I insisted that the children would benefit from my message. The child insisted on returning Sunday evening through Wednesday and wrote me a short note. *"This is the first time I ever understood preaching, my name is _____*, my daddy is the pastor."* She was 9 years old and had missed hearing her father's sermons because of the children's program and missed the messages of visiting preachers because her father hired a sitter to stay with her during all evening services because she had to rise early for school.

No wonder so many children are eventually lost to the church.

---

*Names omitted to protect the guilty.

When will we learn that children are strong, bright and can clearly understand the message of Grace when the Holy Spirit conveys the meaning to their open and believing hearts? Faith-based operations should be aware that Spiritual Formation normally takes place by age eleven. After this target age, the hill is much harder to climb. Neglected exposure to the foundational elements of faith could easily delay spiritual development or cause one to reject God's mercy and grace. Parents and adult believers must give priority to the spiritual formation in children. Perhaps, in addition to family worship and study in family devotions, the anointed homily of the Pastor would be the key that unlocks the door to faith and the sure practice of a moral and ethical lifestyle. Early exposure to the anointed speaking from the pulpit may made a drastic difference in a child's future.

The sharing/learning process in conveying subject matter can best be explained by a connection with those desiring to nurture others or deal with problems and functions which impact individual listeners in their audience. The action steps taken to nurture growth and address life related problems by sharing relevant subject matter has value whether the speaker is a parent, coach, mentor, minister, educator or academic researcher. The intent to transfer valued information or guidance to increase the knowledge base is a noble venture and should be respected and encouraged. Although intention is a primary indicator that differentiate secular, sacred and scholarly, some may attribute different forms of influence to sharing subject matter.

Normally, understanding the dichotomy of general and specialized knowledge and the difficulty of listening and learning requires either a concerned parent, a dedicated teacher or concerned faith-based person sharing hope and grace which leads to changed lives and a broader and more positive view of the future. Since listening and learning are functions of the complexity of the human brain and beyond the basic awareness of many, it is explained in different ways. Here is a baker's dozen of possible explanations:

1. Learning is acquired through personal experience, study, or shared data, information and facts that can be used to answer questions or solve problems in the process of creating new data in the knowledge base.

2. Learning is a change in disposition or capability by external stimuli, and not attributed to natural human development or physical growth.

3. Learning is long-term change in knowledge or behavior based on the memory function of the learner.

4. Learning is based on feedback, consideration, and development when information is internalized and mixed with what is already known which influences changes in thinking and behavior.

5. Learning is difficult to define because it is used to reference acquisition of new and the mastery of existing knowledge which becomes an extension and clarification with experiential meaning and is an intentional and organizing process of personal assessment of relevant concepts and constructs.

6. Learning is simply the process of gaining new information for the knowledge base that adds expertise to enhance life and work.

7. Learning is building on one's present knowledge base and strengthening some and weakening other responses by adding new information to the memory.

8. Learning is a process of acquiring actionable facts which enhances the present state of knowing to connect data and information and enable better understanding and more focused behavior.
9. Learning occurs when one enhances their performance potential and doors are opened that were previously unknown.
10. Learning is acquiring information and skills that are presently used or stored for ready access when the need or opportunity arises.
11. Learning leads to positive change in both mindset and behavior.
12. Learning enables one to correct the inferior before constructing the superior in many aspects of life and vocation.
13. Learning is a never-ending process, a kind of snowball effect with each journey around the sun.

Thomas Aquinas (1225-1274) was a priest and an influential philosopher and theologian. His famous quote on faith is appropriate here "To one who has faith, no explanation is necessary; To one without faith, no explanation is possible." In his account of the learning process and the general acquisition of knowledge, Aquinas described two basic principles: sensory perception and cognitive-intellectual power. The starting point for the acquisition of knowledge was in the external sensory powers which included sight, hearing, smell, taste, touch and the internal senses of common sense, imagination, awareness, reason, memory and intuition or instinct and what some have called estimative powers. Aquinas believed all learners possessed an intellectual/cognitive power which exceeds the external sensory powers.

Obligations of a Speaker

Acknowledge prior study as vital to active learning.
Advance dialogue response to subject content.
Arrange for feedback and/or open dialogue.
Assume that individuals learn in various ways.
Display the significance of advance preparation.
Encourage informed participation of an audience.
Promote ways for sharing among learners.
Provide time for listeners to share on the subject.
Recognize the sophistication of communication.
Respect audience prior experience and knowledge.
Share expectations and learning outcomes.
Stimulate to excite and direct the self-activity of individual listeners.

Exposure to external stimuli, the brain may receive useful information, but this data must be utilized to benefit the individual. Gathered information must be analyzed and absorbed in the memory and used quickly. If the subject matter is not assimilated through the learning process and applied to current questions or problems, it will vanish and may eliminate other unused facts from the memory bank. To be exposed to data, facts or information that are not put to functional use is a double loss. Time and energy have been wasted and the opportunity for observable growth has been neglected.

The known aspects of subject matter sharing are a small part of the professional process; the primary endeavor, aside from scholarship and serious study, is working with others. Many expressed concepts and constructs are based on limited observations, weak assumptions and a lack of experiential knowledge of communication. Passive spectators just do not have the same perspective as active participators. It is as different as being on the bench or on third base with a chance to score for the home team. For example, the reluctant congregant for the Sunday sermon or the unprepared student in the Monday classroom who did no homework or advance preparation will observe only *"the tip of the iceberg"* and miss an opportunity for a Titanic lesson in listening and a proper response to opportunity. Learning the lesson that *"opportunity equals obligation"* usually comes with the shock of a grade report or the adult loss of career advancement because of limited knowledge. Either way, neglecting any learning opportunity may have negative consequences.

The intense labor and preparation for the delivery may never be known or fully understood by those who should benefit from the content of the message, the facts of the lesson, or the new knowledge presented in research findings. Without expressed interest and advance preparation, one does not become an informed participant or an open-minded listener ready to learn. Unanswered questions and emotions are unnaturally strained because of a lack of two-way involvement. Not necessarily dialogue, but certainly the advance awareness of the topic and the willing reception of content which brings answers or understanding to a life situation that may be expressed even non-verbally.

There is clearly a non-verbal component to all communication and interaction between two or more parties. Behavior and elements of speech, aside from the words, transmit meaning. Non-verbal communication includes pitch, speed, tone, volume of voice (or PA system), gestures facial expressions, body posture, stance, proximity to the listener, eye movements and contact as well as dress and general appearance. Some speak of paralanguage illustrated when a one hears the familiar phrase *"don't use that tone of voice with me."* Sarcasm is when the tone conveys an opposite message than the words. A less obvious aspect of paralanguage includes speed, volume, and pitch and duration of speaking. Best explained by a family visiting a new church and were seated near a portable speaker of the PA System. The small child whispered, *"Mama, why is that man hollering at us?"*

    Human behavior is classified in four basic personality types: optimistic, pessimistic, trusting and envious. Clergy may be confident and expectant of faith-based listeners, classroom teachers may be distrusting and suspicious that students are seeking short-cuts, and researchers are presuming that transferred primary data will be received and reported honestly. Speakers as well as writers, demonstrate their attitude and personality type in their presentation of material. It is a transparent quality that is not easily hidden, and it disturbs their communication and limits audience understanding because of the possible distraction of personality. A writer is taught to put himself in the background and a speaker must be guarded and restrained and beware of possible predisposition to act or respond with over-confidence, and too aggressive or hard-hitting in making a point. This is not easy for a strong personality. The speaker must behave similar to an actor and get in character and speak with the voice of the source material. Authority is in the source of the material not in the personality of the speaker.

Lack of Influence: Is the speaker a leader with the ability to influence others to follow voluntarily toward stated objectives? Does the speaker fall into the common trap of being only an arranger of facts, information and data without relevance, energy, excitement or practical applications of subject matter? Does no linkage exist between prepared data and real-life situations? Is the instructor only concerned about sharing prepared facts with little attention to the "take home value" of the presentation for the audience? Did the speaker lack influence to get the audience to listen, learn, retain and use shared subject matter? Does the speaker emphasize action over listening to the facts? Any of the above may have a negative impact on listening and learning.

An individual with a PhD in Communications was hired to accompany me to several preaching events. To my surprise, regardless of the speaker, the presentation, or the location, the observations were the same: *There was no content only an effort to solicit an immediate response!"* At first, this was considered a mistaken perspective by an academic. However, interaction with communication specialists brought seven (7) points of understanding:

1. Content was lost in the appeal for action.
2. Appeal for action drowned out the purpose.
3. Desire for visible response overpowered content.
4. Response usually misunderstood by the speaker.
5. Non-verbal feedback were not considered valid.
6. All non-verbal response were generally ignored.

7. Only physical response was considered valid

A Varig Airline Stewardess, who spoke both Portuguese and English, was secured to accompany me to the fastest growing congregation in South America. The congregation was in Rio de Janeiro, Brazil. Plans were to make notes in English and compare them with the Stewardess notes in Portuguese. The outcome was most revealing. Selected observations regardless of language knowledge were placed on a common list:

1. The congregation owned a radio station and a printing press, but no church building.
2. The church rented the third floor of a public building.
3. The people cued up a block and half at service time.
4. Each one had 3 books: purse, songbook, and a Bible.
5. The pastor stood up and greeted the audience and shared a humorous comment and everyone laughed.
6. The audience sang a well-known Gospel song Then they received an offering and everyone participated.
7. The pastor shared a New Testament parable.
8. The people were challenged to behave the Message.
9. Everyone stood at closing and the pastor walked down the aisle praying for each row. When he reached the door, he closed with a firm Amen!
10. When I opened my eyes only three people remained in the room: the pastor at the door, myself on one side, and the Varig Airline Stewardess on the other.

11. The Pastor shared the time of the next service to be after lunch about 2:30 pm.
12. Me and the Stewardess went to lunch and returned for the afternoon service.
13. It was totally different. The pastor asked for response to their witnessing during lunch and in each section someone stood and introduce one or more individuals to whom they had presented the possibility of a changed life through faith. The pastor himself introduced three new converts and announced a firm date for baptism, new member instruction, and fellowship and training meeting for the new members.
14. In the follow-up with the Stewardess notes in Portuguese, and my non-verbal notes in English (not knowing Portuguese) correlated almost 90%. Her Portuguese notes gave *Chapter and Verse for the story,* where my observation was, *he turned to the back of the Bible and shared a Parable.* She gave the *name of the Hymn* and my notes simply was *they all sang an old hymn.* It was clear why this congregation was the fastest growing church in South America at the time. What can the worship leader, the pastors, the membership learn from these facts? **What did you learn?**

The communication of subject matter is similar regardless of the person, place, process or pattern used in delivery. Preparing to speak or teach and the sacrificial expending of time and energy are never fully known or appreciated by learners or church congregants. Was there concern for evaluating responses and follow-up guidance for use and application? In faith-based operations, the congregation often assume that God freely gave the words of the message through some spiritual anointing to the speaker; however, God does not bless ignorance, laziness or the lack of preparation. Clyde Reid wrote the book, *The Empty Pulpit*, because research showed no one was listening. The same is true of an unprepared teacher when students receive no lasting value for *"time in class."*

Early in a pastorate in South Carolina, a young man with some obvious limitations often sat on the front seat during the Sunday morning service. He had a unique memory for a short period. After the service, this young man would often go to the front steps of the church and repeat the last 15 minutes of my message word for word. These were the days before recorders were in common use. My rush out the side door and around to the front door was not to shake hands with the congregation but to hear the young man repeat the climax of my message. It was most inspirational. My spirit is always lifted by a good Sunday homily.

All social communicators must be aware of John Milton Gregory's laws about the transfer of subject matter: the speaker must *know the material to be presented* and the learner must attend with interest in the subject. The teacher must *stimulate interest, arouse a spirit of enquiry, and get the learner involved.* Provided all speakers followed these constructs, it would advance the proper use of social communication strategy and personal benefit and public good of subject matter sharing. An audience or class would clearly understand the "labor of love" involved in preparing to share data, facts, and information designed to nurture, guide and increase the known knowledge base of others.

Categorically Omitted: Before we get the notion that untrained and uncredentialed individuals are categorically omitted from sharing subject matter, a check with sacred scripture may provide useful information. At times it appears that God has "other ways" of getting an important message to listeners and onlookers. Benjamin Spock in his book, *The Common Sense Book of Baby and Child Care*, told a teenage mother, **"You know more than you think you do!"**

Here are some events from my book "SO TALES" which illustrate when qualified individuals fail to communicate necessary truth, God will find a donkey to speak to a prophet (Numbers 22:28-31), or rocks to cry out when the people fail to speak (Luke 19:40), or a breeze in a mulberry tree to give a message (1 Chronicles 14:15), *uncultured and uneducated men,* (Acts 4:13) who are able and willing to speak transparent truth to the needy.

The Jawbone Story: Careful preparation was made by a young minister scheduled to speak to a national youth convention in the 1960's. The conference theme was *"Use what you have!"* Most delegates were teenagers and the effort was to challenge them to use what they had in hand to *"fight the good fight of faith."* He spoke about how young David had used five stones to win the battle against the giant, Goliath, how Shamgar used an ox goad to kill 600 Philistines and save Israel, and how Samson used the jawbone of an ass to kill 1,000 of the enemy. At this point, being aware of the teenage audience, careful effort not to use the word "ass," caused a Freudian slip where the unconscious thoughts overrode intention… "donkey" was to be substituted for "ass" but this is how it came out: ***"Samson took the jawbone of a donkey and beat the ass off a thousand Philistines!"*** You guessed it; the teenagers rolled in the aisles. It was the Sixties when the vocabulary of faith-based young people was severely limited.

The audience of teens had never heard a minister speak about *"beating the ass off somebody."* They exploded in laughter. With youthful ignorance came frustration. Turning to the man in charge with a puzzled look, he simply said *"close the meeting!"* This we did, but the laughter continued and so did the story of my Freudian slip.

Many years later, having lunch with a Florida couple, he told the story of someone speaking at a youth convention and getting his tongue on his eye teeth and saying, *"Samson took the jawbone of a donkey and beat the ass off a thousand Philistines."* Gail sheepishly asked, *"Did you know that was Dr. Green?"* We had a good laugh. Of all the stories told about my early ministry, Gail's Grandmother enjoyed the jawbone story most. She lived to be ninety-two and asked me to tell her "the jawbone story" many times. It was the kind of slip of the tongue that both young and old enjoyed. After the initial embarrassment, sharing the story myself became a joy. In fact, on her death-bed Grandmother Parks asked me to tell her again the **"jawbone and donkey story."**

Without listening and learning there will be no legacy.

Chapter 5

Message and Dialogue

The messenger is a vehicle, the channel or instrument through which subject matter is shared, yet, the authority is not in the messenger, but in the source of subject matter.

The source of content is the real medium of the message together with the trustworthiness of the speaker. Marshall McLuhan, a Canadian philosopher, wrote a classic *The Medium is the Message—An Inventory of Effects* (1967). His work had great influence and my appreciation for some of his thinking grew; however, the message of this book is different. The medium is not the message, in fact, neither is the messenger the medium. When the medium is considered the vehicle or the instrument by which the message is delivered and the message is considered the meaning or intent of content, the source content of the subject matter must be approached from an exhaustive effort to validate origin and authenticity.

As a teaching/pastor, a ministering/professor, or an academic reporting research findings, the issue of messenger vs. message may become clouded. Nonetheless, the messenger is a vehicle, the channel or instrument through which subject matter is shared, yet, the authority is not in the messenger, but in the source of subject matter. The unassuming and self-effacing behavior of John, The Baptist, clearly illustrated his expression of unworthiness to even loose the sandal straps of Jesus. He was a voice in the wilderness, but the words of the message were *"The eminent coming of the Messiah."* (John 1:23) and were sourced from (Isaiah 40:3) and preserved in a sacred text document.

Speaking in a Community Church near Baltimore on the subject of *"Living a Separated Life,"* each time the point was made that God expected believers to live a clean, separated and holy life, an old brother in the back would stand and say *"Call him John, Brother."* Being new to dialogical response to the message, it was confusing trying to figure out what the old gentleman meant. Finally, it dawned on me that this was a community church and the audience included several denominations. Perhaps this man was an old Methodist who was taught the doctrine of Sanctification

The next time the message reached the phrase, *"God expects believers to live a clean and separated life,* I added, *the old Methodists called this Sanctification."* At this, the old man jumped to his feet and said, *"If his name is John, call him John!"* He was coaching me to use a theological term "sanctification" instead of only describing the results of a sanctified life. He became an informed participant and it all came out OK.

The old gentleman got me to use an old theological term "sanctification" with at least thirty-two (32) meanings being avoided in favor of sharing the practical meaning in application to living a clean and separated life. We both won what was not a battle, but a **two-way dialogical response** in basic communications of the central thought of the message. Getting the listener involved was working whether the interruptions were appreciated or not.

It is at this point that one must differentiate between sanctuary speaking, classroom teaching, and reporting research findings in a lecture hall. Just as Jesus, the Master Teacher, had authority, integrity and credentials, yet He was not the message, but the Voice present to read the message as an intermediary. The **source of the message** was in the Words of the Sacred Scroll trusted by the synagogue audience and presented in a sacred place. The message was shared and received as coming from an authoritative and documented source in addtion to the qualification, certification, and integrity of the voice. A flawed speaker may muddle the message with bias, unsound logic or inappropriate application until the sourced data becomes meaningless. However, when properly sourced and shared in an acceptable manner the message will be received and valued.

Why did Jesus stand to read and speak in the Synagogue at Nazareth where He lived as a child? The authority was in the sourced words of the Scroll available in the synagogue. Jesus was the vehicle, but the Words of the Scroll were the message. Could this be why a minister stands to speak, but a Judge, having a seat of authority, makes a decree or judgement based on written laws while seated. A major concern for the speaker is to make sure the audience understands the source and significance of shared subject matter. This must be discerned and respected so the audience clearly knows the authority of the message is sourced in respected preparation and the reliability of the messenger is secondary and transitional, however, trusted content comes either from a documented and trusted source, the first-hand knowledge of a researcher, or from sacred writings which according to (1 Peter 1:25 EDNT) *the Word of the Lord continues perpetually and is the message you heard.*

Social communication is about introductory steps that lead to useful information related to family, career, and a positive future. An objective of this book was to open the treasure trove of data on the sharing of subject matter by proper exposition and instruction or first-hand explanation of research findings regardless of venue or presenter. It does not deal with "soapbox" feelings from an improvised platform for informal or spontaneous speechmaker as an outlet for delivering *opinions* which are often unsupported by logic and reason.

Language is part of the problem. Obviously, words have their true meaning in people and these meanings change with circumstance, culture, time, place, and location. *(The words "Play Ball!" could be used and understood in any game that uses a ball).* Yet, from the history of word origins, and how culture and time have shaped their actual meaning, the essence of words imbedded in the past and the tracked changes in the maturing of language may be determined by serious study. It is assumed that the fundamental nature of a speaker's words is interpreted by a measured personal understanding in the contextual use of language based on origin and culture of both listener and speaker. Unless the audience has prior knowledge of the subject matter, understands the speaker's words, and attends as an informed participant, little listening or learning will occur regardless of the validity of the subject matter or the qualification of the speaker.

The changing dynamics in communication theory clearly impacts the sharing and learning process. Sharing may generally be classified by intention and methodology or generalized by location, speaker or subject matter. However, the need for preparation and the principles and methods by which information is conveyed to listeners and related directly to basic communication principles.

The objectives of information sharing are clear: accurate facts, a stated purpose and a realistic structured within basic communication concepts. The intent and function of subject matter sharing by location and speaker may be the only definable differences with many more similarities. Human activities within the social professions are not always observable or easily divided by the ways and means of sharing. All speakers must stimulate interest in the subject, arouse a spirit of inquiry by the audience and excite and direct their self-activity related to the subject, which includes analysis and action to assure listening and learning.

Although public education has countless books to guide teachers and professors, two good books for speakers and faith-based audiences were Clyde Reid's *The Empty Pulpit* – A Study in Preaching as Communication; and James Braga's *How To Prepare Bible Messages* - classic gifts of grace to speakers and listeners. My early exposure to Reid's work about communication and Braga's clear and logical method of preparation were sound guidance for my clergy/ teacher function. Through the years the essence of their constructs has remained a trusted source for communicating subject matter through books, classroom teaching, sanctuary speaking and research reporting.

Later as a Graduate Professor of Education and Social Change, concepts received from books and teachers became an integral part of my preparation to share. Whether teaching a seminary class or an advanced student in Graduate School, it became obvious when either authors or books were endorsed, the volumes seem to disappear from the library. It became noticeable that honest students could carelessly become good "book-keepers." Through the years it became necessary to purchase used books to replenish the library or make books available to students so they could return their "borrowed" copies to the course reserve section of the library collection.

There are three formal ways to convey subject matter content to an audience and one basic delivery methodology. The three approaches are:

1. **Thematic** — relevant subject-based emphasis;
2. **Exegetical** — key word-based subject focus;
3. **Descriptive** — simplify complex material.

How does this proceed?

An introductory subject-based emphasis should be relevant and establish a foundation for learning more. The key word-based focus explains building-blocks and developmental constructs of the subject, while a descriptive approach is a simplification process to explain essential subject areas and encourages further study. The delivery method for all approaches to formal sharing is based on the steps of the teaching/learning process: (1) stimulate interest in the subject, (2) awaken a disposition for analysis, (3) energize and direct the self-activity of the listener, and (4) clearly explain to the learner procedures to learn more in the subject area.

A descriptive interpretation may explain a segment of subject content, the relevant subject must be introduced with emphasis and a word-based focus should develop the essential elements of the subject. All forms of public speaking require speakers to be "unashamed workman:" Braga stated: *"No amount of knowledge or learning or natural endowments can take the place of a fervent, humble, devoted heart which longs for more and more…"*

All subject matter sharing goes beyond preparation and delivery. The presentation is more than spoken words it goes to the integrity of the content source and the qualifying preparation of the speaker. A sanctuary homily may be the witnessing of a teaching minister and be enriched by a personal missional lifestyle. The classroom lesson is valued by the qualification and personality of the teacher. The reliability of research findings is validated by the academic standing and integrity of the investigator.

Basically, there are a variety of approaches to conveying subject content and despite the noticeable difference in construction and delivery, all use methods of exposition to explain content in the transfer process of sharing. One type introduces the subject or topic from a particular source, but may use other resources in developing the topic from a common unit of data that structures an outline and adds related information from key word sources to explain the intent of foundational issues or critical interpretation of content based words from one particular source to explain difficult areas in a concise and organized manner and simplifies the meaning to the specific level of the audience. A consideration of age, grade-level or advanced education and culture is the basis for the selection of vocabulary and colloquial expressions.

Knowledge-based Sharing

A properly prepared and presented delivery involves a two-way *emotional identification* between speaker and the audience.

1. Knowledge-based sharing involves **advance preparation.**
2. Knowledge-based sharing involves **content analysis,**

   A study of the intent of specific words and determining the best way to communicate the original intent in the common language of the audience.

3. Knowledge-based sharing involves **word-based analysis**

   A qualitative method to create structure to interpret, describe and share the characteristics of an expository unit of data.

4. Knowledge-based sharing involves **contextual analysis**

   Placing the data within the original historical and cultural setting to better understand the meaning of words.

5. Knowledge-based sharing involves **focused analysis**

   Using the principles of hermeneutic interpretation to determine the beneficial significance of data.

6. <u>Knowledge-based sharing involves</u> **dogmatic analysis** to

   Break down the parts and uncover interrelationships: a kind of language algebra to "reconnect the fragmented parts" to better grasp the primary meaning.

7. <u>Knowledge-based sharing involves</u> **empathetic listening;**

   Paying attention to the speaker and seeking to understand the content and both the specific and general meaning. Without concerned listeners, no benefits are apparent.

An example is the foundational documents of a Republic, known as The Constitution, Bill of Rights, or the Declaration of Independence. Such papers are worthy of respect and should not be disparaged. This is the broader sense of sacred.

The sharing/learning process is similar whether it is information shared in a faith-based sanctuary, a public classroom or reported in a lecture hall. Although the nature and grounds for acquiring knowledge is a primary indicator of intention which differentiates sacred from secular, some may attribute different objectives and intended influence in various aspects of information sharing. In reality, almost every forward step taken by the human race is based on either sacred or introductory knowledge passed forward through faith-based or educational channels to the present.

My professional beginning was as a novice and there were needs for lots of meditation, study, and work to become equal to the pull toward helping others. Every opportunity was taken to advance my education and gain practical experience. As a young man traveling and speaking to youth groups was exciting. At every opportunity there were discussions about my speaking with anyone of experience. Learning along the way, but the hardest lesson to learn about my early sharing of scriptural content came from a mature pastor in Seaford, Delaware.

At the end of a five-service youth emphasis, the senior pastor asked me to stay a few days to discuss my ministry. It was an opportunity to learn ways to improve my preparation and presentation in public speaking. His constructive criticism was that my memory enabled the quoting of too many verses of sacred writings which often confused the young people.

> [This mystified me: how could the quantity of sacred writings be a negative influence on young people about their life and future?]

His explanation was clear: *"When you are older and more experienced you will be able to give more time to explaining the meaning of words rather than just reciting verses from memory."* He warned: *"it would be better if you shared the essence of the passage and the location and applied the meaning to their lives."* Worthy instruction and constructive guidance from a mature professional improved my approach to preparation and delivery of future speaking.

From that moment forward, every opportunity that came my way to learn from any available source was taken with joy. First, a bachelor's degree in Biblical Studies, then a seminary degree in Divinity, a master's in Religious Education, a doctorate in Theology with an emphasis in Greek exegesis, and a university doctorate in Philosophy in the field of Education and Social

Change. My desire was to add quality content to my speaking, but my formal study never replaced the sacred writings that informed my life and purpose in speaking.

In fact, a Texas church member who worshiped in a church near a seminary where visiting Professors were frequent speakers, complimented my approach to sharing complicated concepts in common language by telling a friend *"He speaks like he doesn't even have an education."* His compliment was an evaluation about expressing concepts and constructs in common language. It was encouraging. Instruction about the philosophy of serving and the sharing of faith-based content was guiding my communication.

Certainly, as quality of content increased more time was used expressing in my own words the original preserve sacred writings to life. Taking to heart the constructive guidance of others, scriptural content remained central to my thinking and preparation to speak. Having more to say was good, but it never replaced the foundational concepts learned from sacred scripture and the constructive advice from friends.

Such shared information relates directly to survival and upward mobility for the future of mankind. The basic aspects of education are to equip others for a vocation and a better life; social research attempts to find a workable path forward, and the mission of faith-based organizations deals with a belief system, morality, ethics, fairness and a transcendent concern for life on this planet and beyond. Human efforts in education intends to develop Individuals into moral and productive citizens of the world, while faith-based groups attempt to aid the transformation of individuals into mystical citizens of better world.

Faith-based operations concern a relationship with a Higher Power, touches on morality to guide personal lifestyle behavior, and conveys meaning for life and death. Sacred matters provide an understanding that physical death leads to an extended existence in the Hands of the Creator. Clergy, teachers, and research professors are all charged with sharing fact-based-data that could prepare individuals for a positive future which includes the rewards for a life well lived. There may be disagreement about the nature and quality of an afterlife, but the human heart intuitively yearns for the reality of an afterlife where individuals are judged by a Creator who made man to glorify God and enjoy Him forever. Those who choose not to accept or communicate these facts in a humane manner are neglecting a large part of their social and professional opportunity. In the mind of many: *opportunity equals obligation.*

According to sacred scripture (Genesis 2:7; 3:19; Ecclesiastes 3:20; 12:7), God made man out of the dust of the earth and breathed into that man the breath of life and man became a living soul. The man was told he would *earn his food by the sweat of his face all the days of his life.* Then after his personal journey on earth he would return to the Hands of Creator for a final evaluation. No wonder school children fear a final exam and avoid many tests in life that would prepare them for the future.

Considering the reality of (Genesis 3:19) that we still *"earn our bread by the sweat of hard work all our days."* Since the first part remains operative, why do we fear the second part *"from dust you came and to dust you will return,"* or embrace the wise words of (Ecclesiastes 12:5-7) concerning life after death: *"then shall the dust return to the earth as it was:* **and the spirit shall return unto God who gave it."** The New Testament many years later gathered together the Old Testament concepts and added a dimension of mercy and grace **"the spirit returns to God who gave it."** Where does faith come into this picture? The first part remains true: *"we earn our bread by the sweat of our face all the days of our lives."* With this reality many centuries later, why not accept the authenticity of scripture?

The big question: *"What comes after man's purposeful expedition on earth?"* This depends on God's evaluation of personal faith and conduct. Was life well lived or was it one of squandered existence?"

The sum total of us must appear before the judgment seat of Christ; that the whole character of every one may be made manifest to receive a recompense for things done in the body whether good or worthless. (2 Corinthians 5: 10 EDNT)

1. Therefore you are without excuse, as a human being passing unfavorable judgment on another, you have condemned yourself; you criticize but do the same things. 2. But we are confident that the content of God's judgment is based on truth against those Who commit such things. 3. Do you think that you will escape the condemnation of God that do the same things you criticize others for doing? 4. Or do you entertain wrong ideas about God's truce, His kindness and longsuffering; not knowing that the kindness of God causes you to turn away from evil and begin a new moral life? 5. But because a hard and unrepentant heart stores up against you God's anger in heaven on the day of God's judgment; 6. when He will settle accounts with each man according to his deeds: 7. and eternal life to those who steadfastly do well and seek glory, honor, and immortality: 8. but to those who are controversial and do not obey the right, but yields to the wrong, a rage of righteous anger, 9. constraint and trouble from the Jews first, and also from the Gentiles, on every soul of man who constantly does evil; 10. but praise, honor, and peace, to every man who consistently does good, to the Jews first, and also to the Gentiles: 11. for there is no partiality or favoritism with God. (Romans 2: -11 EDNT)

17. The time is ripe for judgment to begin with God's house: and if our turn comes first, what will be the end of those that disobey the gospel of God? 18. And if the righteous are saved narrowly, what chance will the godless have? 19. Wherefore let those who suffer in accordance with the will of God, entrust their souls in well-doing to the Creator who is trustworthy and true. (1 Peter 4:17-19 EDNT)

Note the thoughts of this Hungarian writer:

-Attributed to the Hungarian writer Útmutató a Léleknek..

LIFE AFTER BIRTH

In a mother's womb were two babies. One asked the other:

"Do you believe in life after delivery?" The other replied,

"Why, of course. There has to be something after delivery. Maybe we are here to prepare ourselves for what we will be later."

"Nonsense" said the first. "There is no life after delivery. What kind of life would that be?"

The second said, "I don't know, but there will be more light than here. Maybe we will walk with our legs and eat from our mouths. Maybe we will have other senses that we can't understand now."

The first replied, "That is absurd. Walking is impossible. And eating with our mouths? Ridiculous! The umbilical cord supplies nutrition and everything we need. But the umbilical cord is so short. Life after delivery is to be logically excluded."

The second insisted, "Well I think there is something and maybe it's different than it is here. Maybe we won't need this physical cord anymore."

The first replied, "Nonsense. And, moreover, if there is life, then why has no one ever come back from there? Delivery is the end of life, and in the after-delivery there is nothing but darkness and silence and oblivion. It takes us nowhere."

"Well, I don't know," said the second, "but certainly we will meet Mother and she will take care of us."

The first replied "Mother? You actually believe in Mother? That's laughable. If Mother exists, then where is She now?"

The second said, "She is all around us. We are surrounded by her. We are of Her. It is in Her that we live. Without Her this world would not and could not exist."

Said the first: "Well I don't see Her, so it is only logical that She doesn't exist."

To which the second replied, *"Sometimes, when you're in silence and you focus and you really listen, you can perceive Her presence, and you can hear Her loving voice, calling down from above."*

The long life of Benjamin Spock (1903-1998) and the popularity of his seminal book, *The Common Sense Book of Baby and Child Care*, published in 1946 (with revisions up to 2004) by Duell, Sloan & Pearce, deals with the urgent search by parents and caregivers for assistance with the problems of growing children. Dr. Spock's first book was simple and had a straight-forward message to mothers **"You know more than you think you do."**

Listening and learning are functions of the complexity of the human brain and beyond the basic awareness of most. All speakers must comply with Gregory's rule about language *which must be common to both the speaker and the listener.* The choice of vocabulary is crucial to the transmission of subject matter. Technical words present a vagueness to an audience unfamiliar with the subject, and such words must be defined and rendered in simple terms to be understood.

For example, when a seminary trained pastor *"the message today is about soteriology and next Sunday the topic will be Pneumatology"* to show his honored position and sophisticated education, there will probably be misunderstanding of the homily. It is unwise to use specialized jargon or technical language without simplification. When a speaker is unaware or deliberately neglects audience awareness of specific language, preparation has been neglected. Listening and learning stops when the complexity and vagueness of sophisticated or technical words are introduced without simplification. This is where an academic must become a scholar and use common words. A speaker's knowledge of the culture, language and general comprehension is key to all forms of communication.

Before Billy Graham became famous and still visiting campuses for InterVarsity, it was my privilege to introduce him to a mixed group of students. The audience was a third Jewish, a third Catholic, a third Protestant and a few hypocrites, but Rev. Graham had prepared well for such an audience. Most were surprised when he arrived for a Religious Emphasis Address dressed in a tennis outfit without any trappings of a minister. After an introduction, he walked briskly to the lectern and began.

Three men entered a restaurant, and each ordered a bowl of soup. One was American, the others were an Englishman, and a Scotsman. When the order came each bowl had a fly in the soup. Each man reacted based on culture and upbringing to eliminate the fly. The American in a relaxed manner casually flipped the fly out; the Englishman took a teaspoon and daintily dipped the fly and placed it on a napkin, then neatly folded the napkin and tucked it under the saucer. Then, the penny-pinching and frugal Scotsman reached into his soup and picked up the fly and said, 'Spit it out; spit it out!' And the audience broke into laughter. After the students stopped laughing, he concluded his brief remarks:

Just as one may act differently in eliminating a fly in their soup, so do individual differences in culture and tradition cause various decisions about Jesus Christ, whom I believe to be the Savior of the world. He closed with a brief prayer, *God bless these young people and enable them to make good decisions in their life and future. God bless you all! Amen!*

Fifty years later at a gathering of alumni, when asked *"Do you remember Billy Graham's message?"* Almost spontaneously the answer came, *"You mean about the fly in the soup?"* Adequate preparation and understanding the audience is key to effective listening and remembering shared information regardless of the speaker or venue.

> The above story about Billy Graham was shared with an early planning group for the 1974 Lausanne Congress on World Evangelization.

Teachers, at times, assume that content is more important than the listening/learning process. The nature of most subject matter sharing, regardless of the pace, place or presenter, is lost because the audience is not prepared with prior knowledge to be an informed participant or have an eagerness to analyze and act on the content of the lesson. Consequently, there is little effort to make real life applications and enable the long-term memory to store learned facts for future use.

Chapter 6

Sharing and Knowledge

"Don't be afraid to trust your own common sense. You know more than you think you do."
—Benjamin Spock

The commonsense key to listening and learning is *"respect."* An unabridged dictionary defines respect *"look at and pay attention to."* Respect for yourself, the subject matter, the speaker then using common words to reach the audience becomes the door to significant learning. Speakers and listeners must use their common sense in dealing with the sharing of quality and quantity of existing and accessible subject matter. There is evidence the audience know more than they think they do, especially those who feel the tug of a call on their life.

The present nature of comprehensive learning is based on an early introduction to subject matter that forms an undeveloped short-term mixing bowl and ultimately when properly used is transferred into a long-term memory bank. This mixing bowl builds on the knowledge base which began in kindergarten and elementary school. This store of information is normally formed by about age seven and most future learning is based on facts stored and recalled from this memory reserve.

Educational entities normally offer general competency levels during the odd years and specialized competency in the even years to assist with application and use of previously learned data. This is to enable learners to take basic facts and apply them to specific tasks as they develop. For example, some academic courses such as math or language require at least two years before credit is granted on a transcript. The facts become clear as each step in the learning process is taken. Each step prepares the student for the next level of learning. This is why it is important that young or new students do not miss any part of the early class orientation or the daily classroom instruction.

The learning progression in subject matter sharing is to enable the listener to adequately analyze and process data, information, and facts with the intention of answering questions and/or solving problems. When questions are answered and problems are solved, new knowledge is formulated and stored in the long-term memory bank. This is the actionable knowledge that will be used in future encounters and involvement in life and careers. This suggests further discussion of short and long-term memory.

The sharing of data, information, or facts does not alone produce knowledge. These items simply are briefly placed in the short-term memory and must be used in a real-life situation or academically to answer a question or solve a problem to become attached to the memory bank. Only information in the long-term memory can be considered stored and useable knowledge provided an adequate recall system is available.

These two types of memory are handled by different parts of the brain. Short-term memory functions in the frontal lobe of the cerebral cortex. However, data stored in the long-term memory is first held in the *hippocampus* and then transferred to the area of *cerebral cortex* related to language and perception for permanent storage and use.

Short-term memory is limited and holds information for brief periods contrasted with long-term memory which has unlimited space when it is finally transferred to the language and perception area for permanent storage. When data in the short-term memory is used, it is transferred to the lower level storage of long-term memory. Data in the short-term memory will be lost unless utilized or relearned, but long-term memory is more stable.

When data in the short-term memory is not used or processed immediately, the memory fades quickly and there is a permanent loss. The long-term memory requires a mechanism of hints to prompt the recall. This is where advance preparation, classroom assignments and homework enter the educational process. Without prior awareness of the subject, the opportunity to use the data, information, or facts becomes limited. There is little hope that any permanent benefit will result from only attendance where subject matter is shared. The rule is *"attend with interest to what is being taught."*

Asking questions is a form of feedback and provides the listener dialog with the presenter. In pulpit or lecture hall events, there is little dialogue and not much learning. In an early pastorate it was decided that feedback from the audience was needed. This is why a "sounding board" group was established to facilitate the feedback and the interactive aspects of learning.

Not fully understanding dialogic response to speaking, the "sounding board" structure was used to provide clarity to the Sunday morning homily. A group (5 to11) members were selected to listen to the Sunday morning message and meet with the Pastor for a brief discussion over coffee or tea. The members were asked to identify the essential elements of the homily and what they actually understood and/or learned. This feedback assisted communication of spiritual concepts, because if this group did not clearly understand the essential elements of the message, the rest of the congregation also missed the significance of the sermon. This would mean the content relating to the message of hope and grace was not received or internalized by the congregation.

In the field of education there are periods of discussion and weekly exams to provide feedback for the teacher. In fact, when a majority of a class does not recall an important aspect of the lesson, the teacher becomes aware of a weakness in presentation. Education would be improved if exams were considered an evaluation of the teacher rather than a basis for assigning a grade for students.

Should one look closely at graduates and their possible use of subject matter content most likely they would discover that much was stuffed into the short-term memory as they crammed for an exam and was lost a short time after unloading on a test. In the process of teaching it was learned that the difference between an "A" student and a "C" student was about one hour. One knew the material before the test and the other learned in the review after the test. Often the "A" student, because of loading the short-term memory (by cramming before and emptying it on the test), did not necessarily retain the information. However, when the "C" student reviewed the material and learned why answers were missed, the process caused a recall system to work and store the material in the long-term memory. Yet, academia will not give the "C" student credit for the learning after the test. This becomes an act of discrimination and does permanent damage to the student. The teacher is to be a facilitator of learning, not hindering the possibility of future growth.

Remembering the words of President George W. Bush when questioned about his time in school, his response *"I am an inspiration for all the "C" students in America."* Recalling a retired Marine Master Sargent in my class after hearing a similar explanation of A and C students, he gained a new self-image and renewed self-confidence. One does not become a Marine Master Sargent without a significant capacity for learning. My experience is that "sergeants" run the military. After class, the ex-Marine shared his renewed self-confidence by saying, *"They always made me feel dumb, but I knew the material and was able to function using the knowledge. My record of promotion verifies my knowledge. Why can't educators understand that students are in school to learn…. if reviewing why a question was missed on a test, doesn't the student now know the answer? Why do teachers not recognize this knowledge and show this learning on the Report Cards? It was learned as part of the process!"*

Some teachers assume that content is more important than the listening/learning process. The nature of most subject matter sharing, regardless of the pace, place or presenter, is lost because the audience is not prepared with prior knowledge to be an informed participant or have an eagerness to analyze and act on the content of the lesson. Consequently, there is little effort to make real life applications and enable the long-term memory to store learned facts for future use. Subsequently, some good students are damaged by the teaching and grading process when their study and review skills worked to gain useable knowledge. Their future function proves the case. I was told by a Yale Professor that the apparent weak students ended up owning the businesses and hired the "A" students as day workers to do the heavy lifting while the "C" student made trips to the bank.

A major weakness and disappointment in subject matter sharing is that most individuals are not persuaded that the facts being shared are good and useful for both the present and future. This is true of most activity in the social professions, but this effort requires a tireless labor of love! In the case of teachers, ministers, or researchers. A good teacher has affection for the learner and personal attachment to the academic subject they present.

The clergy usually have a personality and nature as a spiritual individual concerned for the welfare of others. Academic researchers have a compulsion to search for solution to problems and find answers to troubling questions. Researchers assume the listener in a lecture hall or the reader of a book have both prior knowledge of the subject and a genuine interest in the significant findings of valid research. The social professions normally have a love for sharing and have verified sources or relevant content on the subject at hand.

The practical imperatives of a well-educated leader, known for speaking his mind and writing his convictions, were preserved in an early letter to the Thessalonians. Paul wrote about the attitude or predisposition of leaders and learners which remains worthy of study. His advice was: **Know Those Who Labor among you.** Paul was the best educated individual recognized in scripture. He had both a Jewish education from the best Scholar and a Roman education as a citizen of Tarsus. He also being raised in a Jewish home was taught the language of the Greek servants. All this prepared Paul for an integrated life and career to reach outside his comfort zone to multiple ethnicities.

> [A point of reference: in God's dealing with mankind there is neither male nor female; however, most of the ancient sacred writings were created in what was then a "man's world." Now things have changed for the better. No damage is done to scripture references if one sees the word "man or brethren" as gender neural and makes a candid rendering to include all believers, mankind or the human race.]

> *12. We request brethren that you know those who labor among you, and are over you in the Lord, and give you special directions; 13. And respect them highly in love for their work's sake. And be at peace among yourselves. 14. We urge you, brothers, warn the idle, comfort the faint-hearted, support the physically weak, be long-suffering with everyone. 15. Be certain that no one retaliates evil for evil to any one; but always pursue that which is good, both among yourselves, and to all men.*

> (1 Thessalonians 5:12-15 EDNT)
> **See expository outline following**

Paul's Practical Guidance
Predisposition of Leaders and Learners

A. <u>Learner's attitude toward Leaders</u>
   1. **Know those who labor among you.** 12. And are over you in the Lord, and give you special directions and 13. respect them in love for their work sake.
   2. **Adjust to the situation.** — And be at peace among yourselves.

B. <u>Leader's attitude toward Learners</u>
   3. **Admonish the disorderly** 14. We urge you, warn the idle,
   4. **Console the fainthearted** — comfort the apprehensive,
      Side-bar: fainthearted could be translated pusillanimous; which means—nervous, timid, fearful.
   5. **Sustain the weak** —support the physically weak,
   6. **Be patient toward all** —show longsuffering with all men. 15. Be certain that no one retaliates evil for evil to any one;
   7. **Always pursue that which is good** —both among yourselves, and to all men.

Laws of Sharing/Learning

Laws form a system of rules defining correct procedure or behavior which may be enforced by the imposition of penalties. While still studying law, John Milton Gregory clearly articulated *Seven Laws of Teaching* in a published book (1884). Two years later he gave up the study of law to become a pastor and a college professor, and administrator, working primarily in Michigan and Illinois, where he organized the University of Illinois. Gregory was buried on the university campus in 1898, but his timeless insights on the sharing/learning process survived and have been a blessing to many in the social professions of clergy and teaching and remain useful today for all who study to share.

A predisposition to give clear and understandable instruction on subject matter to others is required in the sharing/learning process. Understanding Gregory's basic rules could create the praise of grateful listeners and will be honoring sacred writings which required all leaders to be *"apt to teach."* The word "apt" in sacred writings clearly expressed being *ready, qualified, inclined, or suitable to teach others by life and lip.*

Neglect the fundamentals and even credentials and subject-specific certification will be useless pieces of paper. Those who attempt to communicate without Gregory's perspective will become frustrated and produce passive aggressive behavior among a resistant audience. In the early drafts of Gregory's laws, he used "pupil" rather than student or learner. What did "pupil" mean at the time? From the Latin, it describes a "little boy or doll" and suggests immaturity of one who needs a teacher or guide. Those who do not effectively teach contribute to the immaturity of a generation and may be responsible for some of the problems that society and religion face because of immature behavior and selfish acts of undisciplined conduct. In the simplest form, Gregory's Laws remain relevant to the needs of learners and can be a blessing to faith-based and fact-based instruction. These laws should be reviewed and practiced by all who wish to inform others on any vital subject. Below is a brief refresher of the wisdom of Gregory:

1. The teacher must know that which he or she would teach.
2. A learner must attend with interest to the lesson being taught. (Gregory placed the responsibility for class attitude and behavior on the teacher.)
3. The language, used as a medium between teacher and learner, must be common to both.
4. The facts to be taught must be learned through facts already known. (The lesson must move from the known to the unknown.)
5. Excite and direct the self-activity of the learner, as a rule telling them nothing they can learn on their own.
6. The learner must reproduce in his or her own words the facts to be learned.
7. At least one-third of teaching/study/class time should be given to basic content learned.

Gregory's Laws expanded:

1. The learning leader/coach/mentor must know the subject matter.
2. A learner is one who attends with interest to the leader and the lesson.
3. The language, used as a medium between teacher and learner, must be common to both.
4. The facts to be taught must be learned through facts already known.
5. Excite and direct the self-motivation of learners, as a rule telling them nothing they can learn on their own.
6. The learner must reproduce in his or her own words the facts to be learned.
    (a) ***Memorization** is the first level of learning.*

(b) After the shared facts are clear there is an elementary degree of **understanding**.

(c) The next step in the process is the ability to **paraphrase** a thought or concept in one's own words.

(d) Finally, the desire to search for **supportive evidence** to support one's understanding is realized, and an effort made to apply what was learned.

(e) **Application** is required to reinforce the learning process.

7. At least one-third of teaching/study/class time should be given to review and/or application of the data to be learned.
   - What does the lesson say?
   - What does the lesson mean?
   - How may the meaning be expressed in my own words?
   - How may my understanding be verified as acceptable?
   - How may the lesson be applied to my life and career setting?
   - What can be done to enable my awareness and expectation to become an informed participant in learning?
   - What process can be used to review and retain the content through better application?

Perhaps a visit to the Garden of Gethsemane with Jesus, the Master Teacher, and a group of sleepy disciples (learners) would be instructive. The disciples were too sleepy to be alert for one hour. Physical weakness does at times challenge the best of speakers in the process of providing vital information to an inattentive audience when even the best listener cannot stay alert. Since Jesus, after three attempts to arouse the sleeping disciples, returned to His meditation, His behavior could be an example for the weary instructor. Finally, Jesus told the sleepers they had enough rest, it was time to face the challenge. Command of the material and control of the learning environment is crucial to preparing individuals for the challenges ahead. A lack of attentiveness creates a difficult situation for the one sharing subject matter. It takes years of experience and patience to deal with the lethargic nature of listeners.

In music a rest note creates a deliberate pause, which is an essential part of the musical structure. Conflict or struggle in any situation suggests the need to take a step back or find a quiet place to contemplate the situation. This provides time for reflection on the present area of concern and opportunities for mature guidance in the process of moving forward. An occasion from my childhood memory of the pastor asking one of the men to wake up a sleeping parishioner when the response was *"Pastor you wake him up...you put him to sleep."* Perhaps speakers and teachers should take responsibility for the attentiveness of their audience. Gregory believed teachers were responsible for the behavior of their students. After all a basic rule in teaching is to *"stimulate interest, arouse a spirit of inquiry and excite and direct the learner to the subject matter."* Inattention could be a fault of the speaker or the listener's preparation to be an informed participant on the subject. This situation is a two-fold problem which could be solved by advance preparation by both speaker and audience.

Music is a good teacher. The value of harmony and a Sunday homily is enhanced by a predisposition to acknowledge the value of the message and a spirit of respect which prepares congregants for the expositional messages that explains a portion of sacred writing. The classic hymns are filled with verses which teach the basics of a faith-based life. The speaking of a respected pastor provides guidance for living a moral life and becoming a positive influence in society. Obviously, the structure of music becomes a preparation for receiving the message of grace. There is an event in ancient scripture where in troubled situation the value of music was confirmed.

There are examples of music serving as a precursor to an improved situation. In time of trouble, the Prophet called for music to create a situation essential to hearing his message. He asked for a minstrel (a singer who player a stringed instrument).

As the minstrel played, the Hand of the Lord came upon the Prophet and inspired him to provide instructions and guidance for the ultimate solution to the current problem. From this incident and the record in 1 Samuel 10:5ff where the inspiration of stringed instruments, hymns and chanted psalms improved the atmosphere for a speaker. *"The Spirit of the Lord will come and you shall speak forth and be turned into another man."* This early record of a prophet being *"turned into another man"* suggests that music is part of the preparation for an inspirational speaker. In the New Testament there is additional confirmation of the value of music in message sharing:

15. Look carefully how you walk, not foolishly, but in the light,.16. Buying up every opportunity, because these are evil days. 17. Wherefore be not reckless, but prudently understand the will of the Lord. 18. Stop excessively drinking wine, which influences riotous living; **more willingly be influenced by the Spirit; 19. but speak to one another in exalted verse, songs of praise, and sacred music, singing and making melody with the music of your hearts, to the Lord; 20. continue giving thanks to God the Father for all things in the name of our Lord Jesus Christ; 21. line up under one another in reverence to Christ.** (Ephesians 5:15-33 EDNT)

Later a similar experience was when my first book was presented to a publisher's book editor. The editor responded: *"The manuscript is over-documented! Mr. Green, do you not have anything to say yourself?"* The editor seriously considered over documentation as a lack of maturity and/or an absence of first-hand knowledge on the subject. *(Another publisher took a chance on the book and with a few changes it sold 30,000 in 90 days: yet an important lesson was learned.)* Fifty-five books later the academic documentation process remains a struggle when expressing acquired knowledge (where did that idea, concept or construct originate, and should credit be given to someone)? Writing a book, *Why Churches Die,* while studying Church Growth at Fuller, and being influenced by the faculty, a dilemma developed: how were my sources to be documented? Finally, it was decided to state: *"In the field of Church Growth my concepts were influenced by Dr. Donald McGavran and my work may have quoted him inadvertently."*

Documentation of Sources: In speaking to PhD students about documentation of crucial concepts in their dissertation, my lesson plan included the honeybee and the gathering of nectar to make honey. The bee worked at gathered a syrupy fluid (nectar) from various flowers and brought it back to the hive and with great effort made it into his own honey. We enjoy the honey without knowing the particular flower from which the nectar came, but sometimes when the hive is near a clover field one can taste the hint of clover. Or near an orchard one gets a taste of the fruit in the honey. In a sense, the bee is documenting where the syrupy fluid originated from the flavor and taste of the honey.

Academic background, professional experience, the books read, and learned behavior all influence writing and speaking. To be overly concerned from which blossom the nectar came, may be left over from a previous generation and can hamper the development of creative material. Asking my son where he obtained his ideas and quotations, his answer: *"I just say a great man once said, then I lean back and say aloud the thought or expression. Then I quote myself."* Of course, this is no excuse for intentional plagiarizing when the source is classic, and the original source may be cited and referenced. Notwithstanding the need for source credit, it does show the difficulty in documentation when the wise man Solomon wrote:

> *8 All things are full of labor; man cannot utter it: the eye is not satisfied with seeing, nor the ear filled with hearing. 9 The thing that hath been, it is that which shall be; and that which is done is that which shall be done:* **and there is no new thing under the sun. 10 Is there anything**

whereof it may be said, See, this is new? it hath been already of old time, which was before us. 11 There is no remembrance of former things; neither shall there be any remembrance of things that are to come with those that shall come after. (Ecclesiastes 1:8-11 KJV)

In writing a Preface for a friend's book, and faced with his lack of documentation, the story of the honeybee gathering nectar was shared. Also, that well-educated and mature individuals, who have spent their lives reading and studying a given subject often *"gather nectar from far and wide and make their own honey"* to the displeasure of academics who wish to enforce a particular discipline of documentation. This is done as if serious students have no creative thoughts or failure to understand that most present information began with a knowledge base at about age seven (7) and has grown ever sense. In qualitative research and in a literature review of relevant data on a subject, most were taught to search for the original source or "first use" of the concept or construct and not to quote a secondary or tertiary reference. There seems to be a lot of Smith who quoted Jones who quoted Johnson who quoted several more back to some ancient source. In the case of *"There is no new thing under the sun."* the original source was Solomon in the Bible.

First Teaching Assignment: Life itself and all experience-based knowledge completes a general field of knowledge constructed in the Knowledge Base initiated early in life. The light of each day and the pain of each problem adds to this memory base and prepares the individual for life-long learning. My Mother's first teaching assignment was a rural one-room school on a lonely mountain with grades 1–8 together in one room. Teaching weak students was a challenge, but a committed instructor will find a way to reach even the slow learners who are trying to participate but have limitations. One value of the one-room school was that no student was ignored or left behind. A willing mind or an opportunity to reach a struggling student is a terrible thing to waste. One must correct the anomaly before the straightened arrow can reach the benchmark target considered to be age-specific education. The one room school was a challenge with all elementary/secondary grades together. It was a challenge for young teachers, but probably the best education America provided for early education.

Explaining the dynamics of the one room schoo, it was clear the fast learners were challenged by listening to the upper-class lessons, and the slow learners were able to review difficult lessons by hearing them taught again to lower grades. Also, the older and smarter students assisted with the younger students. Everyone benefited from the process. Individuals were prepared for life and higher education in the one room school. In fact, the entrance exam given to eighth graders for access to high school was one that many college graduates could not pass today.

Mother shared that one boy in her class seemed to read diligently when the group read aloud, but he never knew the material. As a teacher, she was concerned and arranged for the class to stop reading at a given signal so she could hear the one student read aloud. She learned why he never knew the lesson: he could not read, but was saying aloud, "Here, Tag, here, Tag, here, Tag..." He was simply calling his dog.

The one room school worked for most students, except those *who spent time calling their dog or for some students who "did not pay attention."* In fact, a remembered excuse given in defense of a bad Report Card, *"I was so poor; I couldn't pay attention."* On another occasion three brothers were late for school on a snowy day and from their clothing they had obviously been playing in the snow. When they finally arrived the oldest boy explained, *"Sorry we are late, it was so slick out there...every time we took a step toward school we slid back two."* Then came the logical question, *"Well, tell us how you finally got to school."* Without hesitation the answer was, *"We got mad and started home."* Mother said she could not bear to punish such a bright young lad. Oh, for the good old days when teachers understood the students and the students were honest and without excuses. In fact, Mother taught me the meaning of an excuse was *"An excuse is the skin off a reason stuffed with a lie."*

Religious Emphasis Week: An invitation to speak at the Religious Emphasis Week at a college where my mother was Dean of Women was a challenge. Concern gripped me because it was one of the few times my mother would hear me speak as an adult. My style of speaking at such events was to understand a scripture passage and then make a candid rendering into common language. Normally, my approach was *"The deeper meaning here is...or the original intent of the language here was, etc."* As the first chapel service progressed, mother turned to a colleague and said, *"He will say things* *that are not in your Bible, but he is a good and honest man."* As I transliterated certain words and gave my free rendering from the Greek, mother turned to her friend and said, *"See I told you he would use words that are not in your Bible."* She was listening.

The Greek Professor. Encouragement came, however, when the Greek Professor understood my approach and shared with his class, *"Listen in chapel and you will understand how the study of Greek is to assist your understanding of language and improve our communication, not to demonstrate your knowledge."* Learning the Professor had made this statement in class was reassurance to continue the process of giving the original intent and devotional meaning of scripture in my public ministry. It began a 42-year journey to expand my Senior Academic Thesis on the *"Development of the English Bible"* by exegeting the koine Greek of the New Testament into a common, devotional language that was true to the original intent of scripture.

Decades Long Journey: The result of this four decades long journey was <u>The EVERGREEN Devotional New Testament (EDNT)</u> – a candid rendering rather than a literal or word for word translation. The EDNT is an effort to place scripture into a more understandable language. The work may not demonstrate a rigid scholarship as would a word for word translation with extensive notes to explain the academic process, but that was not the objective. This is because the Greek word order and many of the "explanations" for translating a passage differently than other existing texts are so academic that the explanations hinder the value of the devotional reading. Some may think it too sermonic, but this work was intended as devotional, not strictly academic. The objective was to make the text understandable and clear to the average reader the same way a pastor attempts to present scripture as part of his Sunday homily. The EDNT text is a candid rendering of my understanding of the Biblical text from First Century Greek Manuscripts.

No Parsing or Commentary: It is my conviction that the original text was in the common language of the people and needed no parsing or detail commentary. When the English Academics transliterated the common Greek into the scholarly language of Shakespeare (1611) much of the original intent was lost to the reader and required long and boring sermonic attempts to make sense of what God intended to be a clearly understood message. No wonder Clyde Reid's (1967) research in preaching as communication caused him to declare the American Pulpit empty (because no one was listening.)

From What Book? Speaking at a national youth convention in Virginia some years ago, my former pastor came up to me and asked, *"From what book did you get that sermon?"* My answer was simply, *"The Bible!"* He insisted on knowing what book, so I said, *"Matthew."* He asked from what book did you get the ideas. Pulling out my Greek New Testament and reading Matthew 28:18-19 to him in Greek. *"That's where I got the ideas!"* It seems that parents and older ministers never realize that young people grow up, become educated, get new ideas, and start thinking for themselves.

The message in question was on what some call the Great Commission as a self-defeating theology of coercion. The weak translation made the Challenge of Jesus into an effort to compel people to *"go and do"* when they were clearly instructed to *"make disciples as they went about their daily lives."* Explaining that the *"go"* of the commission was really a participle and not an imperative and should be translated *"going"* or *"as you go"* was the foundation of the message. Jesus gave His followers instructions to follow: *"as you personally go into all the world make disciples."* The challenge was for believers already in motion, the power to "go" was in their believing hearts. In fact, Jesus asked that they *"wait in Jerusalem until"* they were fully enabled by the Spirit to share the message of hope and Grace with those they meet on their journey. Yes, there would be struggle, but regardless of the hardships, the end was worth the journey!

They did not need ministers to challenge and push them toward involvement. They needed only to be encouraged to practice a missional lifestyle. The pastor's question suggested that old preachers never believe that young men can become scholars and teach them a new perspective. As young speakers begin to think for themselves, the family, the community, faith-based worship and positive social change has a chance at renewal.

Hermeneutics and rhetoric are an essential part of preparation and delivery of a written or spoken message.

Chapter 7

Pulpit and Classroom

A distinction between a sanctuary homily and a classroom lesson: the homily is for a personal life-change, and classroom instruction is about earning a livelihood and changing the world.

How and why the subjects of hermeneutics and homiletics became associated exclusively with clergy training is not clear. Both have Greek origins and grounding in *linguistics* which is the study of human speech including nature, structure, and changes of language. *Hermeneutics* includes the principles of interpretation and *homiletics* has to do with address, speech, conversation, and association. The other question: why was the study of rhetoric dropped from study? *Rhetoric* is the art of effective or persuasive speaking or writing and has to do with compositional techniques. On the other hand, *homiletics* is the study of preparing and delivering a prepared manuscript.

The concerns of *hermeneutics* are the rendering of the intent of the original use of particular words presented in language that an intended audience would understand. While *homiletics* deals with the preparation and delivery of a homily, speech, message, discourse, lecture, lesson or report in any venue or format.

It is my firm conviction that all who deal with sharing subject matter could profit from the study of *linguistics* including hermeneutics, homiletics and rhetoric. The concepts and constructs of these include knowledge needed by all who share content with others. One needs the basic knowledge of these disciplines to be an effective communicator. Preparing a manuscript, studying for a homily, structuring a research report, or preparing to teach in a public classroom, all must use the science of *hermeneutics* (interpretation of the root meaning of words.) Once the original intent of the words is determined, the presenter must find a way to render the meaning in common terms the audience will clearly understand.

The venue of a sanctuary differs greatly from the lecture hall where academic competency based on personal research is presented or in a cohort classroom where a qualified and experienced teacher with specialized competency in the sourced subject is valued. The construct of dialogue should be understood as interchange, exchange, or discussion from any means to supply feedback and make application from readers or listeners relative to a particular manuscript or discourse. Dialogue will improve the compacity to understand and learning will enhance application of knowledge by those who read carefully an article, report on a book; and a listener who gives dutiful and respectful attention to a speaker then analyzes and appropriately applies that which was learned.

An old Deacon was asked the difference between the clergy's sanctuary homily and the teacher's lesson in a public classroom. He saw the difference in simplistic terms: *"Teaching is speaking in low gear, while the sanctuary homily is teaching in second gear."* His perspective was related to the speed of delivery rather than actual function or structure. Perhaps from his viewpoint, a traveling minister, such as Billy Graham, may be speaking in high gear or popular televangelist may be speaking in overdrive.

Since Clyde Reid's, *The Empty Pulpit* (1967), on preaching as communication, and the definitive work of James Braga, *How to Build Bible Messages* (1968), and my work dealing with thirty-five reasons *Why Churches Die* (1972), drastic changes in local faith-based groups have continued. In the Foreword,* Donald A. McGavran, Major Professor in Church Growth at Fuller, wrote about the decline of the American Church and the abject failure of the membership to fulfil their Commission.

>*Note this excerpt from Dr. McGavran's **Foreword** in *Why Churches Die*
>
> *Many denominations in North America have ceased growing. Some are declining. And this at a time when less than half the citizens and the youth are practicing Christians. Though the population is expanding, thousands of congregations are smaller now than they were a few years ago.*
>
> *Even worse, during the past war decades church growth has often been regarded as materialistic, base, and even disreputable. Derogating growth, evangelism, and the very church itself is fashionable in some quarters. Those who rightly stress that Christians should love mercy and do justice, often erringly assert - or imply - that only ethical action is true and relevant Christianity. While churches sicken and die, while two billion have not yet heard effectively the name of Jesus Christ, whole denominations spend almost all their resources on things other than discipling men and women.*
>
> *By way of contrast with all this, Dr. Hollis L. Green recognizes the growth crisis and addresses this book directly to it. He knows the American church well. He speaks to real conditions. Wasting no time on superficial...*

The progressive weakening of faith-based groups, has continued and the pace hastened by neglect and encroachment of unprepared and neophyte leadership. The general public is convinced faith is no longer relevant. The door has been opened to Milton's, *Paradise Lost*, and there is chaos in organized religion, definite pandemonium in the streets, and the few remaining in the sanctuary are not listening to the sanctuary homily.

Preaching and teaching are not juxtaposed in sacred writings or generally compared by academia. There seems to be a "great fixed gulf" between the two in the public arena. Sacred writings support more similarities than academics observe. No comparison or evaluation exists between teaching and preaching in the New Testament, but both seem to be part of the same process. The evaluation and quality in academics appear to be related to the levels of education: college, seminary, graduate school, and post-graduate studies. Some use only two classifications: secondary and higher education. Both are obvious parts of a common process in sharing subject matter with others. Notwithstanding, shared aims, the primary differences in teaching and preaching relate to preparation and delivery, speaker and venue, attitude and aptitude, education and credentials, capacity and suitability of the language used in subject matter sharing. A bi-vocational pastor who teaches elementary school will obviously use different language on Sunday than in the classroom.

There were seeds planted early in life that pointed me toward leadership in youth work, pastorates, church supervision, and a teaching career as a Graduate

Professor in Education and Social Change. My early commitment to patriotism briefly sidetracked me to the Air Force War College and a short-term Reserve Chaplaincy during the Vietnam era. However, the dreadfulness of a shooting war during the Tet Offensive of 1968, caused a reassessment of my faith-based path of ministry through education. Yet, the experience shaped a large part of my professional life and my understanding of world order and conditions of the disadvantaged.

A primary consideration is verbal and non-verbal language, because they both are essential aspects of communication. To attempt to clearly differentiate teaching and preaching is problematic and creates misunderstanding and may engender prejudice and partiality among the immature. Speakers and writers must use language and a style of expression that includes the proper choice of words based on culture, education and the audience. A functional distinction may be found in the grammar moods of the English language*, but these are secondary to the process.

> *Moods refer to a verb category or form which indicates whether the verb expresses a fact (indicative mood) a command (imperative) a question (interrogative), a condition (conditional) a wish or possibility (subjunctive). Teaching is mostly in the *indicative* mood and preaching is generally in the *imperative* mood. However; the process of subject matter sharing may require asking questions (*interrogative*), and may deal with conditions (*conditional*) or speak of hopes and dreams for the future (*subjunctive*).

A speaker must have a grounding in preparation and delivery. These are required to develop meaningful instruction with a methodology that approaches and attracts listeners and supplies a smooth transfer process. Content must be moved in a sequential and cumulative manner that reaches a conclusive or implemental end for application by the audience. This cannot be done without complete knowledge of the subject and grounding in the procedure for transferring information to a particular audience. To complete the process there must be a willingness to listen with observant skill and openness to particular dialogue and audience feedback. The mindset of a coach or mentor is an excellent asset together with the ability to tell a good story to maintain interest and capture non-verbal feedback.

A speaker must be a good narrator, in a manner appropriate to the venue and audience, with the mindset of a coach or mentor with no extra verbiage or jargon. The stance, dress, and assertiveness will provide the listener perspective on the talent, capacity and fitness of both the message and the messenger. The speaker's attitude and aptitude to listen will be transparent and is either sad, weary, agitated, harried or happy for the opportunity to speak. The audience must be content, expectant, listening, and respectful of the speaker. What does *respect* mean—*to look at and pay attention* (all other factors being equal).

Other aspects of listening and learning are controlled by ethnicity, tradition, custom, back-ground, values, belief and personal philosophy. The concepts and constructs of analysis and synthesis together with the corresponding logic of deduction and induction impact both speaker and listener.

Analysis and synthesis together are a kind of language algebra where words represent concepts and constructs that enumerate a commonsense meaning. Analysis breaks the composition into parts for assessment and synthesis puts the parts back together for a better understanding. This language algebraic produces a more orderly comprehension of information into a balanced and usable mix.

There is a "me" and a "we" aspect for both speaker and audience in the speaking and learning process. The speaker's preparation time is "me-time" where books and teachers have made available the data, information and facts needed for the speaker to adequately prepare and present the subject; it is now up to personal initiative and study habits to complete the process. The audience also has a "me-time" which requires preparation to become an *informed participant* and an excited and self-directed learner willing to gather each tidbit of useful data from the message that is relevant and applicable to their lives.

Both the speaker and the audience have a "we-time" when they speak and listen with mutual concern both sending and receiving information in both directions. Usable data for the present and operative facts for the future become the sacred mystery of listening and learning. The "me-we" dichotomy of speaker and audience in preparation and delivery is a significant part of transferring subject matter from speaker to listener and securing feedback from the audience.

The distinct aspect of preaching and teaching is not clear in the sacred record. Neither are definitions or explanations provided by most groups consistent with scriptural exegesis. This causes confusion as to whom the system will allowed to speak in a formal setting; that is, from the pulpit in the sanctuary of a house of worship or the public classroom or academic lecture hall. Some believe that women have the right to share subject matter in many venues, but categorically deny* their right to present a homily from the pulpit. Have we forgotten *"in Christ there is neither male or female?"* (Galatians 3:28)

> *Note: Paul used a different word (1 Timothy 2:9 -12) for "teach" than Jesus used (Matthew 28:19). Paul used *didasko* (without a definite article) his use of (anarthrous-- *present infinitive active*) the mood when distinctions can be made about time and action. His meaning was about a relationship between a wife and her husband and that there was to be peace and quietness in the home. The unit of scripture deals with the wife's conduct and behavior primarily in the home and that she was to learn from her husband discreetly with respect to his position. It is a theological stretch to extend this statement to the teaching or speaking in a public or sacred gathering.

During the first hundred years of the early Way for followers of Jesus, there were no dedicated buildings for gathering similar to present day churches. Also, much of the sharing was conversational in small groups or shared in homes, the marketplace, passed on the wayside, or in *ad hoc* gatherings in a Jewish Synagogue that presented an unscheduled opportunity to share.

> *24. Wherefore the law was a truant officer to keep us in school and a teacher's aide to guide our learning until the True Teacher, Christ, came that we might learn justification by faith. 25. But after faith came, we no longer needed a truant officer or a teacher's aide. 26. For we are all the children of God by faith in Christ Jesus. 27. For as many as have been identified with Christ by baptism have been clothed with the attributes of Christ. 28. In Christ there is neither Jew nor Greek, bond nor free, male or female; for you are all one in Christ Jesus. (Galatians 3:24-28 EDNT)*

Normally, the word "preach" in the Greek New Testament was *kerusso* which referred to various kinds of sharing, announcing and proclaiming in different settings.

When a man healed by Jesus announced his blessing to the city, Mark used the word *kerusso* (Mark 5:20) and there was no evidence of a formal religious service. The Translators of *kerusso* in the New Testament used various English words other than "preach" to announce news or emphasize instruction and explanation rather than only proclamation. The Septuagint, a Greek version of the Old Testament, also used the word *kerusso* in an unrestricted way.

The early letters preserved in the New Testament normally used preach and teach without distinction. (Acts 5:42, 28:31; 1Timothy 2:7; 5:17; 6:2). Old cultures are used by sectarian sections of Christianity to departmentalize teaching and preaching in an attempt to proscribe roles and positions in institutionalized and formal gatherings.

Actually, when both words are considered in their unabridged intent, one cannot preach without teaching or teach without public statements which declare available truth. Consequently, there are many similarities in sharing subject matter. In fact, all early leaders were challenged to be *"apt to teach;"* that is, *suitable and inclined with the mental insight to adapt their work and witnessing to sharing the message of love and grace with others.*

When Jesus gave instruction to His followers after the Resurrection, they understood they were to personally travel and "teach" (*make disciples)* by reaching and teaching all inhabitants in their native homeland or culture. The Spirit promised by Jesus (John 15:15f) was to enable their outreach after the Spirit was poured out at the Jewish Harvest Festival on the group gathered in unity. It was to a small group of Galileans. This did not mean the present church was to be only homogenous and refuse to diversify and branch out to meet the needs of other groups. In that day, cultural constraints, limitations of travel and language caused mostly kinship and common cultural gatherings. At the event called Pentecost, those who came to witness the excitement heard the wonderful words of God's grace within their culture and native language. It was clear that God intended speakers to reach beyond cultural and language differences and share good news to all. Have we forgotten that *"God made of one blood all mankind"* and *"in Christ there is neither male or female"* (Acts 17:26-31; Galatians 3:28)?

The clear message of the Harvest Festival at Pentecost was to share the news of mercy and grace with the whole of God's creation. Everyone was to be reached in the context of their culture, traditions and language (Acts 2:1-11) and gathered into groups for fellowship and guidance. This clearly speaks to "harvest time" and the spiritual enabling to share knowledge and experience with individuals and seeking groups, (Matthew 28:18-19) This writer finds no designation that women should not or could not be fully involved in sharing true facts and basic experience with others regardless of the venue.

In His instruction Jesus used the Greek word, *matheteuo*, with the grammatical construction *(aorist imperative active)* meaning *continuous action that must begin immediately (active voice)* and was *distinguished from the middle (selfish) voice and the passive voice.* This form of "teach" was *to make listeners into learners attached to their teacher and able to share with others;* and thus, advance knowledge to all nations. The "going" was to "make disciples" without selfish reasons and using all forms of sharing including lifestyle witnessing and personal teaching and sharing the declaration of faith.

Those who learned the lesson of faith were to be taught and identified by baptism with the Authority and specific function of the Trinity and instructed to observe all the personally directed commands of Jesus. They were to continually gain experiential knowledge to enable their consistent walk until they arrived at the doorstep of Heaven.

According to Paul, those who provide oversight must be *"practiced in teaching"* (I Timothy 3:2) and leaders of the local gathering must be *"apt to teach"* (2 Timothy 2:24) and all believers were to witness to others at all times by word and lifestyle. The challenge of Jesus (Matthew 28:18,19) instructed His followers to "make disciples *(learners).*" It appears that teaching is an obligation of all mature and qualified individuals as they grow in grace and knowledge.

Paul was born in Tarsus and was named Saul and raised as a Jew in the Roman culture. His education was both as a citizen of Rome and by the traditional methods of Judaism. Education in ancient Rome was important and progressed from family-based to a tuition-based system where wealthy families paid Greek tutors to educate their children. Even poor boys were taught to read and write. Obviously, a Roman Citizen of Tarsus, received an excellent education. In the case of Saul, his religious instructions were in the Jewish tradition and culminated at the feet of Gamaliel. (Acts 22:3)

Gamaliel was a Pharisee and an advanced teacher of the Law, who must have been influenced by the lifestyle of those who followed Jesus because he later spoke out against condemning them to death (Acts 5:34-39). His concern for the followers of Jesus must have come from a deep place in his heart which caused him to pass inadvertently to his student, Saul of Tarsus, while sharing the strict and aggressive teachings of the Pharisees.

This slight concern for others as a Pharisee became a redeeming factor and perhaps an unconscious influence on Paul after his conversion. His perspective of dealing with opposing points of view and troublesome people would normally be from his culture and past education. Although it is easy to still see a hardness in his dealing with stubbornness and transgression in the lives of some for whom he was responsible.

Jesus of Nazareth came to save mankind and make them moral citizens of the world before they became mystical citizens of His Heavenly Kingdom. Yet, Saul of Tarsus, known as Paul, an Apostle to the Gentiles, shaped the congregations of his day and established for the future the functional effort to win all available individuals who would believe and behave the Word and walk the straight and narrow way. Using both intellectual and spiritual insights based on his education and a changed relationship with God, Paul desired local gatherings and individual believers to follow the teachings of Jesus and his common sense guidance in their work within their cultural location and at all future opportunities. As an example, Paul expressed this expectation for gathered believers. Perhaps some of these constructs were influenced by his parents and the moderate teaching of Gamaliel (Acts 5:34)

By All Means Save Some

19. For though I am free from the authority of all men, yet have **I made myself servant to all, that I might win more converts, 20. and with the Jews I lived as a Jew, that I might win Jews to Christ; to those under the law, I put myself under the law, that I might win them; 21. to those without law, as without law, (being under the law of Christ,) that I might win them that are without law. 22. To the weak I became weak, that I might win the weak: I am made all things to all men that I might by all means save some.** *23. I am still doing this to advance the gospel, so that I may become a joint-partaker of the gospel with you.* (1 Corinthians 9:19-27 EDNT)

The Just shall live by Faith

14. I am under obligation to the Greeks and to the Barbarians; both to the wise and the foolish. 15. As far as I am able, I am ready to preach the gospel to you at Rome also. 16. For I am never reluctant to preach the gospel; for it is the power of God unto salvation to all who believe; to the Jew first, and also to the Greek. 17. For in the gospel God reveals His worthy activity that begins and ends with faith: <u>the permanent and authoritative character of the written word affirms</u>, *the just shall live by faith.* (Romans 1:14-17 EDNT)

The word "teach" Jesus used to instruct His followers to personally proceed into all the world with the message of grace is clear. Tragically, this concept and construct is lost through leadership failure and believer's disobedience. Present believers upwardly delegate the individual challenge to congregational leadership. Individuals abandon personal responsibility and assign to a few the tasks meant for all. When staff does most of the field service and handles all the difficult tasks within an assembly including administration, fundraising, management, outreach, in-depth teaching, plus the pulpit ministry, the Challenge of Jesus for total involvement is abandoned. One can predict trouble ahead.

Actually, when leadership does service that others could do, they rob individuals of participation and growth. Yes, the layfolk will greet the visitors, sing in the choir, say public prayers, share in the offering, give a gift for missions, and hold title to elected lay positions without full commitment or concern for obligations. This is partly caused by upward delegation to staff and by leaders who do not delegate.

> *11. And He gave some to be messengers, some preachers, some missionaries, and some teaching pastors; 12. for the **ultimate purpose of equipping the saints for the work of serving,** for the building up of the body of Christ: 13. until we all attain the same faith, and the experiential knowledge of the Son of God, unto mature manhood, unto the full measure of development in Christ: 14. that we no longer behave as young children, driven before the wind of each new teaching, by the trickery and sneakiness of men, whereby they ambush with deceitful schemes; 15. but arriving at truth in love, you may grow up into Him in all things,* (Ephesians 4:11-15 EDNT)

The primary task of clergy is a teaching/sharing ministry plus public proclamation of moral and ethical guidelines, while others do their part in order to free the anointed ones for prayer and ministry of the Word. The stated tasks of all believers is clear: as they personally travel daily on their earthly journey *they are to make disciples, sponsor converts for scriptural baptism, and continually teach those willing to listen to the teaching and the personal responsibilities Jesus designated (recorded in Luke's Gospel and noted in (Acts 1:1-8) to enable them to practice the presence of Jesus daily on their journey to the Gates of Heaven.*

> *26. Look at your calling, brethren, not many of you are wise by the standard of men, not many from the ruling class, not many are called of noble parents: 27. but God has chosen the average to bewilder the wise; and God has chosen the weak things of the world to amaze the strong; 28. and the poor of the world, and the insignificant, hath God chosen, and God gave an affirmative vote to things which are not, to bring to naught things that are: 29. that no human pride could boast in His presence.*
> (1 Corinthians 1:26- EDNT)

There is some overlap of the sanctuary homily and the lesson presented in public classroom. Although both have similarities, there are differences. Instruction in a classroom deals with fact-based data in the context of a structured class and curriculum. Teaching shares correct subject matter, but the atmosphere and context have a different feeling and quality. Paul taught in a church school at Antioch (Acts 11:26) for one year. He also taught as a bi-vocational teacher in the Lecture Hall of Tyrannus* in Ephesus (Acts 19:9) for at least two years and reminded students of previous teaching and used a word meaning *"to provide instruction in a formal setting."* (2 Thessalonians 2:15) It appears that teaching in a school was less emotional than speaking in a synagogue. The work of formal teaching is less announcing and more learner oriented. Instruction is mainly the classroom style of imparting and applying meaningful facts. The classroom provides more opportunity for feedback which is normally missing in a sanctuary homily.

> *History records Tyrannus as a Greek teacher of philosophy and rhetoric.

Researching isolated words that were used for both preaching and teaching. They were merged and alphabetized and a survey instrument constructed. Those who took the survey were told to assign words either to preaching or teaching or both. To view the results or take the survey see Appendix A.

admonishing,
advising,
advocating,
applying,
caring,
clarifying,
coaching,
comforting,
communicating,
0concludin,
confronting,
correcting,

counseling,
edifying,
encouraging,
evangelizing,
exhorting,
explaining,
exposition,
expounding
illustrating,
instructing,
lecturing,
listening,

mentoring,	sharing,
moralizing,	speaking,
motivating,	storytelling,
persuading,	training,
proclaiming,	tutoring,
reading,	writing,

It appears some see little difference in the nature of sanctuary speaking and classroom teaching, the results were predictable: only 4 were marked only for teaching: *[advising, advocating, mentoring and tutoring]* and 6 scored exclusively for preaching: *[confronting, evangelizing, exhorting, expounding, illustrating, and proclaiming]* while the balance of 26 terms were scored for both preaching and teaching: *[admonishing, applying, caring, clarifying, coaching, communicating, concluding, confronting, correcting, counseling, edifying, encouraging, explaining, exposition, instructing, lecturing, listening, moralizing, motivating, persuading, reading, sharing, speaking, storytelling, training, and writing.]* This supports the assumption that sameness exists in the two functions. Difference seems to relate to subject, assignment, venue and the personality and intent of the speaker.

Ichabod and The Holy Television Café

A child was born in ancient Israel at the time the Ark of the Covenant was taken away and the child was named *Ichabod* meaning, *"The glory is departed."* (1 Samuel 4:21) A sign "ICHABOD" over the door of a closed church was appropriate because the glory was departed. Perhaps a secondary sign over the Church

Kitchen, "Kitchen Closed – Cook on Strike" would inform the public there were no more free (fellowship) meals.

One might as well burn the theology "cookbooks" because all the old church folk are eating fast food specials at the Holy Television Café. The cafe serves up exotic and newfangled heterogeneous dishes. Oh, the Holy Television Café has on the set wall a framed color picture of Jesus, a painting of The Last Supper, a couple of old stained-glass windows with images of Saints, and a framed copy of the Ten Commandments. The folk who eat there regularly seem to have strong religious feelings.

They have special meetings on Wednesday evening and Sunday mornings and the Head Waitress serves a carefully concocted communion brew to the regular attendees. How could the concept of a historic place of worship for family and friends become a gathering of strangers at an electronic feeding trough known as the Holy Television Cafe?

Who of my generation would have believed it could happen? Yet, phenomenon is explained in terms of downgraded both proclamation and teaching, discarding Hymnbooks for electrically projected lyrics, or singing by a recorded keyboard rather than the organ, deafening PA box speakers, coffee and donuts instead of fellowship, and commercial-type projects for fundraising instead of tithes and offerings. Sunday school that does not teach anything, no new converts, less participation, and a growing gap between pulpit and pew.

However, the minister remains behind a lectern speaking to *"God's despised few."* Many religious eating places have become various forms of the Holy Television Café on city street corners and the front yards of members decorated with sculptures of saints and icons and idols from the past. It appears the people are viewing life through a rearview mirror with one eye and seeing an out-of-focus future with the other. I join with abandoned John's urgent plea from the desolate Isle of Patmos, *"Even so come Lord Jesus!"*

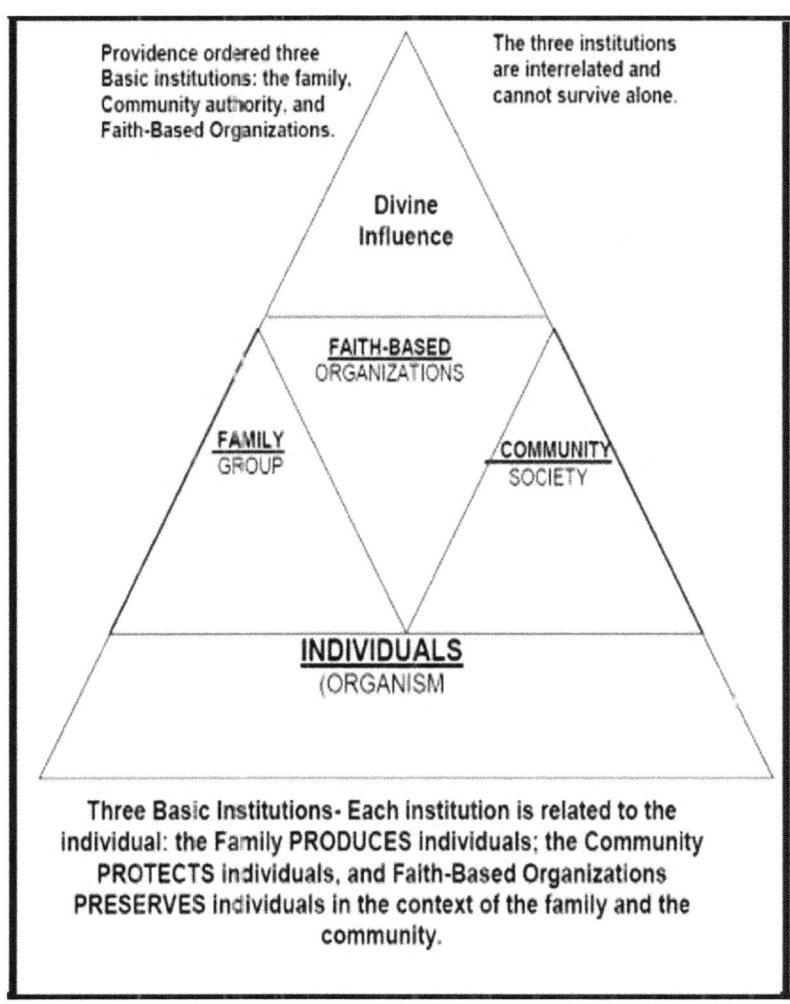

1. Who will be the audience for the subject?

2. Why are they participating?

3. What do they already know on the subject?

Chapter 8

Preparation and Delivery

All subject matter sharing must be organized around a central idea with connected objectives to hold the structure together.

When considering the presentation of material in a sanctuary homily, the regular instruction of a qualified teacher in a classroom or the report of academic research findings, there are only small differences in the preparing and delivering of the verbal aspects of subject matter transfer. Persons in the social professions who become principal speakers and writers have a specialized career path they follow to reach their professional standing. The clergy have a call and faith-based education, plus special training to gain the qualification for ordination. The classroom teacher began with an interest in learning and completes a specialized course of study to qualify for certified credentials. Those academics who do social research normally have graduate degrees with years of experience before they attempt to do social scientific research, write a book, report the findings, or structure a course based on their personal research and investigation. Yet, there is much more about ministers, teachers and researchers that most do not understand or even want to know.

Preparation and delivery are two parts of conveying subject matter. One should never speak or write to a general audience but must be specific as to whom the content is directed. The intended receiver is an essential part of the purpose/thesis which guides the presenter. **Who** will be the audience for the subject? **Why** are they participating? **What** do they already know on the subject? Is the preparation and the planned delivery appropriate for the venue? Awareness of and interest in the subject plus a readiness to participate and learn are required of all receivers. Attentiveness and interest are advance work for the listener. Both the presenter and the audience must be prepared and grounded in the essential areas of communication.

A first level understanding of the science of hermeneutics, homiletics and rhetoric are indispensable parts of preparation and delivery of a written or spoken message. Since all levels of individuals are called to serve, a serious study of interpretation, expression and speech-making could assist many and greatly benefit their audience. Using these tools to improve preparation and delivery could place the difficult parts of subject matter sharing in a more understandable and acceptable structure for an audience. It would also assist the understanding of complicated and sophisticated material in the classroom and the presentation of research findings in the lecture hall.

One must be studious in the disciplines of hermeneutics and homiletics to be an effective communicator. Preparing a manuscript or subject study for a homily, research report, or teaching in a classroom are required. The knowledge of *Hermeneutics* (interpretation of the root meaning of words) would benefit anyone. Once the original intent of words is determined, the speaker or writer must find a way to render the meaning in common terms the audience would clearly understand. *Hermeneutics* is the rendering of the intent of the original use of particular words presented in language that an audience would understand. While *Homiletics* deals with the preparation and delivery of a homily, speech, message, discourse, lecture, lesson or report in any location. *Homiletics is preparing and delivering* a subject-based presentation to a specific venue.

There is a difference in the presentation and delivery of subject matter content by the various social professions. The research reporting academic depends on credentials, position, and expertise. The public classroom teacher follows a stated curriculum for which the instructor has certified competency. Tragically the specialized training received by most clergy is sectarian which creates a biased theological position on most subject matter content with an unquestioning audience. This sectarian bias is clearly defended by the brand names on the buildings, but members of the public are uninformed as to the details and cannot personally evaluate the quality of information shared by local clergy.

It is obvious that a Professor doing specialized research on a subject has credentialed support for such an endeavor. Normally, an audience will trust their reported findings. Formal certification is required for a classroom teacher to be employed to instruct at a specific intellectual level. Also, church goers have expectations of certain competency for ordained clergy speaking from their pulpit even though the specifics of the preparation are generally unknown by the audience.

My dissertation for a Doctorate in Theology discovered that the essential doctrine of a denomination could be rejected by the membership simply by the way pastors presented their opinionated position on the subject. Assuming that the nature of the Call to Ministry and the practical experience of preparing to speak in a faith-based setting was a life changing venture, my second dissertation for a PhD in Education and Social Change, exposed the weak study habits used by pastors in preparation for their regular speaking opportunities.

A review of current and related literature declared that pastors should study but the methodology or process to guide them was never explained. It was determined by a comparison between pastors who spent at least twenty (20) years in a pulpit ministry based on whether they had attended seminary and been exposed to sectarian positions and the teaching of hermeneutics and homiletics. In eighteen (18) areas of comparison between seminary trained clergy and bi-vocational pastors without formal seminary training, there were only two of the eighteen areas where significant difference occurred. Seminary trained ministers generally used Bible language definitions and current event illustrations while non-seminary preachers used dictionary definitions and Biblical illustrations in their effort to add meaning to their message. In summary:

1. Seminary trained pastors used current event illustrations while preachers without exposure to seminary hermeneutics and homiletics used Biblical illustrations.
2. Seminary trained pastors normally used Bible language definitions for words while pastors

without seminary training used dictionary definitions to determine word meaning.

How did this research inform my ministry through education? Basically, that the regular process of teaching/preaching was a training ground for communicating serious subject matter. In real life the process of learning how best to present a faith-based message was by trial and error. Pastors normally went with what worked for them or they patterned their ministry after a former pastor. Since pastors with twenty (20) years of ministry after seminary were compared with pastors with the same experience without seminary training and differed in only two of eighteen intentional areas of preparation, it was assumed that both compared groups obviously developed their ministry through an on-the-job process. It was further assumed the process required regular study and development for the sanctuary homily and other opportunities to exercise their teaching skills necessitated serious study.

Those involved in providing faith-based and/or fact-based information would be assisted provided all the facts are clearly understood. For the clergy what was originally written in common language that required no parsing or explanation must now be simplified. An Epistle was read to a gathered audience then passed to another group. (Colossians 4:16) There were no additional words needed for explanation: it was their mother tongue. The use of parables/stories about real life and personal circumstances and experience were the primary application of the teaching/preaching process. However, the written Word was so clear when read in their Mother Tongue that all were able to understand both the obvious meaning and the application to personal lifestyle and family conduct. If a lack of understanding existed, the people were encouraged to discuss the matter at home with a mature believer.

Likewise, the teacher must be sufficiently aware of the author of a textbook or a collateral text required for student reading to be able to simplify the jargon into the common language-level of their students. Any further clarification should be worked out in the homework assignments to assure understanding.

Being told as a teenager, *If you are planning to be a preacher, travel to Memphis and observe Dr. Lee's Ordination Service.* Yes, I hitchhiked to Memphis and witnessed an ordination. Dr. Lee called the Candidates to the stage, sat husband and wife in chairs and faced them holding a gift Bible and said, **"This book is a message from your Father, read it to your blind brother!"** It was obvious the blind brother would easily understand his Father's words. With gratitude the lesson learned was received and a practical study to understand and explain words in simple terms became a part of my learning and sharing.

Although homiletic and hermeneutics are considered tools of faith-based presenters, these disciplines were originally a part of rhetoric, the study of persuasive writing and speaking used by classic writers, early educators and speakers in many fields of knowledge. Hermeneutics is the science of interpretation and discovering the original intended meaning of a text as it would have been understood by its original audience. Homiletics is a study of public speaking and attempts to carry the original meaning across time to provide meaning and significance for a contemporary audience.

These are classic scholarly endeavors for all writers and speakers. A study of hermeneutics and homiletics would be useful to anyone desiring to improve writing and speaking in any aspect of subject matter sharing regardless of their field. One does not have to be a scholar: homiletics and hermeneutics are tools to assist in analyzing words and content for better understanding. Hermeneutics and homiletics study can be effective support tools for those who share subject matter in any venue.

Homiletics has historically integrated teaching and rhetoric, which includes both writing and speaking persuasively. However, Karl Barth, a Swiss Reformed theologian influenced by Hegel, Kierkegaard, et.al., considered preaching to have a different motive than rhetoric. Barth claimed that preaching should not use stylistic devices or tools of persuasion; consequently, he believed that homiletic and rhetorical should be studied separately. Paul's description of his preaching seemingly agrees with Barth and others:

1. And, brethren, when I came to you, it was not with rational eloquence or wordy cleverness. I made a solemn proclamation concerning the witness of God. 2. I deliberately decided my message among you would be nothing, but Jesus Christ crucified. 3. The method was to process the message in weakness, fear, and much trembling. 4. **And my speech and proclamation were not with persuasive language or subtle arguments based on man's wisdom,** *but in the manifestation of*

> *power by the Spirit: 5. my motive was that your faith should not rest in the wisdom of men, but the power of God.*
> (1 Corinthians 2:1-5)

A Sectarian Position: Notwithstanding, Barth's resistance to *"persuasive language,"* his perspective may have been influenced by a sectarian position relative to rhetoric in preaching. Paul himself was both eloquent and persuasive when it was the best way to present the truth, especially when he spoke at a center of Greek intellectual center and discussed matters with locals in Athens.

> *22. And standing in the center of the Areopagus, Paul said, Men of Athens, I perceive that in all things you are fearful of deities. 23. For as I passed through your city and saw the objects of your worship, I found an altar inscribed, TO AN UNKNOWN GOD. The One you unknowingly worship, I announce to you. 24. The God who ordered the universe and all the things in it, the One being Lord of heaven and earth does not dwell in hand made shrines; 25. neither is He served by human hands, as though He needed something from man, seeing He gives to all life, breath, and all things; 26. and has made of one blood all nations of men who dwell on the earth, determined the history of nations and their territory;* **27. so they should search for God and hopefully find Him although He is not far from all of us. 28. For in Him we live and move and have our being; as certain also of your own poets have said, For we are also His offspring.** <u>*29. Since we are the offspring of God, we ought not to think that the Deity has any similarity to anything made*</u>

of gold, silver, or stone that is sculptured by the art and imagination of man. **30. Then God over-looked this past lack of knowledge, but now commands all men every-where to repent: 31. because he has set aside a day in which he will judge the world with justice by the Man He has chosen and has provided assurance to mankind by standing Him up from among the dead.**
(Acts 17: 22-31EDNT)

Paul also used Rhetorical Questions:

12. There is no difference between the Jew and the Greek: for the same Lord over all is abounding to all who call on Him. 13. For everyone who calls upon the name of the Lord shall be saved. 14. How shall they call on Him in whom they have not learned to believe? And how shall they believe in Him of whom they have never heard? And how shall they hear without a messenger? 15. And how shall they proclaim, except they be sent? As it is written, fully developed are the swift feet of those who proclaim the glad tidings of the gospel!
(Romans 10:12-21)

Apollos was known for his excellence and persuasive speech:

24. And a Jew named Apollos, born at Alexandria, a learned man and mighty in the scriptures, came to Ephesus. 25. This man was instructed in the way of the Lord and with burning zeal, spoke and taught diligently the things of the Lord, though he knew only the baptism of John. 26. And he began to speak boldly in the synagogue: when Aquila and Priscilla listened to him speak, they took him to their house and explained the way of God more completely. 27. And when he expressed

a desire to go into Achaia, the brethren wrote, encouraging the disciples to receive him: on his arrival he was most helpful to those who had believed through grace: 28. and he powerfully and publicly confronted the Jews, showing by the scriptures that Jesus was the Christ.
Acts 18:24-28

4. remembering your tears, I greatly desire to see you again, that my joy might be full; 5. when I remember the genuine faith that is in you, which dwelt first in your grandmother Lois, and your mother Eunice; and I am convinced dwells also in you. 6. For which cause I remind you to fan the flame of the gift of God which is in you through the laying on of my hands. 7. For God has not given us the spirit of cowardice, but of power and of love and self-control.
(2 Timothy 1:4-7 EDNT)

My great uncle, Bill Curton, was a Methodist circuit riding preacher. In a small church on his rural charge in a rough and tough mountain community, the young men were always pulling pranks on the traveling preacher. One time they hooked an old mule to the corner support pillar of the old frame church and during the sermon, they pulled the post out. This caused the small frame building to lean sideways. On Uncle Bill's next circuit visit to that place, he brought a 12-gage shotgun and a pistol. He placed the shotgun against the pulpit and laid the pistol next to his Bible and said, *"I came here to preach!"* And so he did without the interruption of pranks.

As a long-distance circuit rider, Uncle Bill wanted a glass of nourishing milk instead of water on the pulpit. He told the elders, *"I may be dry, but I don't want to be under nourished."* The next Sunday those same boys spiked his milk with mountain white lightning "moonshine." The story goes that as Bill preached, he took a sip of the spiked milk and remarked, *"My God! What a cow!"* Before the long sermon ended, Bill asked if he could buy this special cow, tie it to his horse, and take it along on his long circuit ride to enjoy *"this special mountain milk."*

The rest of the story. Sharing this account in a publication, a Japanese student, Isao Ebihara, sent an email asking, *"What kind of lightning did they put in that preacher's milk?"* It appears that everyone in the world doesn't know about mountain moonshine or the **atmospheric electrostatic discharge** that accompanies the ingestion of such home-made whiskey brewed in the mountain moon light. Notwithstanding, the influence of mountain moonshine is a poor substitute for the Holy Spirit in any respected homily.

During a Sunday sermon, a pastor noticed a dog in the aisle. He called for the deacons to *"Throw that dog out of the House of God!"* After the service a lady spoke to the pastor, *"You shouldn't have put that blind man's dog out of the church."* The preacher went straight to the visitor and apologized. The visitor's response, **"Oh, that's O.K. that sermon wasn't fit for my dog to hear any way!"** This analysis was the visitor's evaluation of both the messenger and the message. The next time, the audience may benefit to reverse the process: *keep the blind man and his dog and find a more sensitive pastor.* Sometimes human nature can get in the way of an honest homily. At other times the straightforward appraisal of a message could be instructive for faith-based leadership.

Provided there is sufficient agreement on both sides of the dichotomy (speaker and listener), conceivably, we could add the study of human relations and ethical behavior to hermeneutics and homiletics for all speakers. This would be a gift to faith-based groups, classrooms students, and lecture hall participants. From my view: this may slow the process down a bit and even hurt a little, but it would bring lasting benefit to speech and communication in any field of endeavor.

The process of educating ministers for preparation and development weekly required messages and delivery them effectively is long and often tedious. During my teaching at seminary, Harold J. Ockenga, as a nationally recognized pastor and educator, was invited to speak to the student body on his system of "Preaching without Notes." He was precise about the preparation process and delivery order. It seems that he prepared one way and unloaded in the opposite order. He preached in series and each week prepared the summary teaching for Wednesday evening first, then the Sunday evening sermon, and finally the Sunday morning message. Then he unloaded in the reverse order knowing exactly where he was going and how far to go in each message. Dr. Ockenga delivered the Sunday morning message first, then the Sunday evening and finally he taught the Wednesday evening Bible study as the summary and crowning achievement of the week.

With Ockenga's preparation plan and the people knowing his approach, listening and learning were increased. His delivery plan stabilized attendance as learners became informed participants interested in the next message in the series. Consequently, with little review of study notes, he knew exactly where the series was going. With only the Bible in hand he could speak with confidence without referring to notes. Obviously, diligence in preparation and knowing the material and his audience, he was able to speak clearly without notes. Compared to the Seven Laws of Teaching, (See pp. 97-99) written by Gregory (1884), the first law being: **"The teacher must know what is to be taught."** Dr. Ockenga's study and presentation plan fully equipped him to know the content and how to best deliver each aspect of the message of faith and grace to the congregation.

The clear and logical method of James Braga in, *How To Prepare Bible Messages,* has been a trusted source for preparing and delivering messages. His method combines effective techniques for public speaking with time-tested theories of teaching. His book provided pastors and message-givers with logical, step-by-step guidance to prepare and deliver effective pulpit messages. Braga thoroughly defines and describes each critical component of a faith-based message from the introduction to illustrations and the conclusion. His work has been a personal blessing and no attempt to improve his work would be made here. His instructions are clear and simple and any person desiring to improve their public speaking could benefit from reading his book.

> *15. Be eager to present yourself approved to God, a workman unashamed, cutting straight the word of truth. 16. But avoid blasphemous and worthless chatter: for they will cause more disobeying of the word. 17. And their teaching will eat as does gangrene.* (2 Timothy 2:1517 EDNT)

Reasons for Serious Study

1. Proclaim the true meaning of subject matter.
2. Present a relevant message application to life.
3. Provide use for basic content of the message.
4. Produce comfort and strength for listeners.
5. Prepare learners for a missional lifestyle.
6. Propagate value of subject beyond words.
7. Promise positive social change and improvement in the structure of family, places of worship, and communities.

The downgrading of proclamation in faith-based messages is more the fault of the sender than the receiver. In a convention of farmers, the discussion would not be about how to get the cows into the barn or get them to eat, but their concern would be *"How do we improve the feed to take advantage of the appetite that always exists."* We learn from this that speakers should be concentrating on the quality and understanding of their source material and making it palatable for those who hunger and thirst for truth and righteousness.

During the time Paul spent in Ephesus, he wrote the first letter to the Corinthians about AD 57. He received reports of factions in the assembly, sexual misconduct, deceptive observance of the Lord's supper, abuse of spiritual gifts, and misunderstandings regarding basic teachings including the resurrection. This letter gave instruction designed to eliminate divisiveness and restore balance to the church. The people's loyalties were divided among Paul, Apollos, Peter, and Christ. God never intended for believers to be spiritually dependent on a man, but on the Holy Spirit and the spiritual fellowship among themselves. This goes to the essence of the faith-based congregation and its function.

1. Paul called by the will of God to be a messenger of Jesus Christ, and Sosthenes, the brother, 2. to the assembly of God gathered in Corinth, to those set apart in Christ Jesus, called to consecration with all those in every place who habitually call upon the name of our Lord Jesus – their Lord and ours: 3. Grace and peace with wholeness and prosperity from God our Father, and from the Lord Jesus Christ. 4. I thank my God always concerning you, for the grace of God which is given you by Jesus Christ; 5. that in every respect you are enriched by Him, in fluency of speech and in all understanding; 6. even as our testimony of Christ was confirmed in you: 7. so that you lack no gift; waiting and anticipating the coming of our Lord Jesus Christ: 8. Who will also make firm unto the end, that you may be without accusation in the day of our Lord Jesus Christ. 9. God is faithful, by Whom you were called into the fellowship of His Son Jesus Christ our Lord. 10. Now I encourage you, brethren, by the name of our Lord Jesus Christ, that you all speak the same thing unto reconciliation and that there be no divisions among you; but that you be joined together in harmony and intentions, 11. It has come to my attention, my brethren, by means of the house of Chloe, that there are quarrels and strife **that ignites a party spirit of contentions among you. 12. This is what I mean: every one of you says**, *I belong to Paul, and I belong to Apollos, and I belong to Cephas, and I belong to Christ. 13. Is Christ divided? Was Paul crucified for you? Were you baptized in the name of Paul? 14. I am thankful to God that I baptized none* *of you, but Crispus and Gaius; 15. lest any could say that I had immersed in mine own name. 16. And I immersed also the household of Stephanas: besides, I do not remember baptizing any other. 17. For Christ sent me not to baptize,* **but to preach the gospel with eloquent wisdom, lest the Cross of Christ should be made of none effect.** (1 Corinthians 1:1-17)

1. Brethren, I could not speak to you as unto spiritually mature men, but as to men with carnal appetites, even as infant Christians. 2. I gave you spiritual milk and not solid teachings: for until then you were not able to digest strong teaching, nor are you able even now. 3. **For you are yet self-sufficient without dependence on God: because there is among you strife, jealousy and party feelings, are you not still controlled by your own nature, and behave as the unconverted?** *4. While you continue to say I am of Paul or I am of Apollos, are you not controlled by men? 5. Who is Apollos: who is Paul, but servants by whom you believed, each doing the work given them by God? 6. I did the planting, Apollos watered; but God caused the growth. 7. So* **neither the planter nor the one doing the watering deserves credit, but God who gave the growth.** *8. Now he who did the planting and the one doing the watering are part of the same process: and every man will receive a reward according to his work. 9. For God is working and the laborers are together: you are God's farm; you are God's field to be worked and God's building to be constructed. 10. According to the favor of God given to me, as a wise master builder, I have laid a foundation, and another will build on it.* **But** *let every worker take heed how he builds on the foundation. 11.* **There is no other foundation for the building but the one laid on Jesus Christ.** *12. The material used to build on this foundation may be gold, silver, precious stones, wood, dry grass and straw;* **13. the quality of each man's work will come to light:** *the daylight will show it, because the day will arise in a blaze of light: and the light shall test every man's labor and building material. 14. If a man's work abides which he has built, he will receive a reward. 15. If any man's work is consumed, he shall suffer loss, but he himself shall be saved; as one passing through fire.* (1 Corinthians 3:1-15 EDNT

1. For you know, brethren, that the good effect of our entering in unto you, continues: 2. but even after cruel and unfair treatment at Philippi, with **Godly fluency in speech we brought you good news with much anxiety and conflict. 3. Yet our appeal to you was not based on false or degraded thinking nor on cunning craftiness: 4. but passing God's scrutiny, He judged us fit to be entrusted with the good news: when we speak, it is not to please men, but God who examines our hearts.** *5. You know that we never used the language of flattery, and God knows we never attempted to enrich ourselves: 6. for we never sought praise from you or others, when we might have been burdensome to you as apostles of Christ. 7. But we were tender among you, even as a nursing mother warmly takes pleasure in her children: 8. so affectionately longing for you, we were willing to share with you, not only the gospel of God, but also well-pleased to share our lives, because you were valued by us.*

> *9. You remember our long and hard labor night and day, because we would not burden you for expenses, but freely preached the gospel of God unto you. 10. You are witnesses and so is God, how upright, honest and blameless was our conduct among you that believe: <u>11. as you know how we encouraged, comforted, and charged every one of you, as a father treats his children,</u> 12. that you would lead a life worthy of God, who has called you unto the glory of His kingdom.* (1 Thessalonians 2:1-12 EDNT)

God still speaks through the written word and through the circumstances of life. There was a time when God spoke in many other and different ways to the fathers of the past, but now He speaks to mankind through His Son and His preserved Word. (Hebrews 1:1-3) The scriptural record shows that God still speaks with *"the still small voice"* of conscience, the wind, the rain, the rainbow, and through the rocks of the earth, or a donkey when the human voice fails to declare His Glory.

Believers are salt and light, God called messengers to bring the Word to everyone who would hear and behave. Through the message of Grace God's servants become a burning and shining light in the darkest places of the earth even the dark recesses of the human heart. When the Word penetrates the heart and opens the hEARt of the soul, **salvation and eternal life becomes available to all.**

> *1. We must, therefore, with special intensity pay attention to things we have heard (understood) and run no risk of drifting away from them. 2. If the word spoken through spiritual messengers was valid, and every violation and infraction of it received an appropriate penalty; 3. how can*

*we expect to escape, if we ignore **so great a deliverance (rescue/safety), that had its origin in the words of the Lord, and then was guaranteed by those who had heard (understood) the Lord's spoken word**, 4. **and God added His own witness by a variety of miraculous powers, and giving them according to His own will, the Holy Spirit.*** Hebrews 2:1-4 EDNT)

33. There is a fathomless depth in God's wisdom and knowledge! His judgments are unsearchable, and His footsteps cannot be tracked! 34. Who can figure out the mind of the Lord? Or who could be His advisor? 35. Who has first given to God that He should pay back again? 36. For God is the source, preserver, and ruler of all things: to God is glory throughout all ages. Amen. (Romans 11:33-36 EDNT)

Sober-minded: *1. I implore you, brethren, by the compassions of God that you place yourselves as a living sacrifice, consecrated and pleasing to God, which is your reasonable worship. 2. And be not fashioned according to this age: but be transformed by a new mental attitude, that you may confirm for your-selves what is good, acceptable, and the complete will of God. 3. For I say this through the grace given unto me, to every man that is among you, not to be high-minded more than he ought to be minded; but to be sober-minded, according to the measure of faith God has given. 4. For as the human body has many parts, and all parts do not have the same function: 5. so we, being many form one body in Christ, and each one is mutually dependent on another. 6. Having gifts that differ according to the grace given to us; if your gift is inspired speech, practice* *according to your proportion of faith; 7. If your gift is serving others, minister well: and the teacher concentrate on teaching; 8. the one who exhorts, must give attention to consolation; he who gives food, clothing or shelter for the poor, let it be done with no partiality; he that governs must do it with diligence; the one who shows compassion must do it with cheerfulness.* (Romans 12:1-8 EDNT)

9. Let love be without hypocrisy. Hate what is wrong. Cleave to the good. 10. Have tender affection for the believers; go before one another as an honorable guide; 11. do not delay your enthusiasm; be on fire in the spirit; serving the Lord as a slave; 12. rejoice in hope; remain steadfast in time of trouble; be persistent in the habit of prayer; 13. contribute your share with reference to the needs of the saints; give attention to hospitality. 14. Bless all who persecute you: bless and curse not. 15. Share the happiness of those who rejoice and share the sorrow of those who are sad. 6. Maintain harmony with one another. Set your mind on high things but accept humble ways. Do not think too highly of yourself. 17. Never pay back injury for injury. Aim to do what is honorable in the sight of all men. 18. As much as you can, live peaceable with all men. 19. Never avenge yourselves dearly beloved but leave room for Gods anger: for it is written, Vengeance is mine; I will repay, said the Lord. 20. There is another test, if your enemy hunger, feed him; if he thirsts, give him drink: for in so doing you will make him feel a burning sense of shame. **21. Never permit evil to conquer you but get the better of evil by doing good.** (Romans 12: 9-21 EDNT)

13. This is why we give thanks to God without let up, because the word of God you heard from us, you willingly welcomed not as the words of men, but as the true word of God who sets in operation an effectual work in you that believe. 14. For you became imitators of the believers in God's assemblies in Judaea who gathered in Christ Jesus, for you also have suffered similar things of your own tribesmen...(1 Thessalonians 2:13-14 EDNT)

A basic difficulty in understanding the
written or spoken word is not the vagueness
of the subject matter,
but the elusiveness of the
writer or speaker.

Chapter 9

Speech and Communication

"A preacher should have the skill to teach the unlearned simply, roundly, and plainly; for teaching is of more importance than exhorting."

—Martin Luther

Effective communication depends on structure. All subject matter sharing must be organized around a central idea with connected objectives to hold the structure together. Having an adequate outline down to the paragraph level assist the writer/speaker in two ways: organization to improve memory and enables the audience to stay focused on the subject matter and follow the logical sequence of delivery. Research has supported that organized information is retained more accurately than subject matter presented without adequate structure. An effective communicator will write and speak based on the acceptable rules of English grammar and the structure of communications.

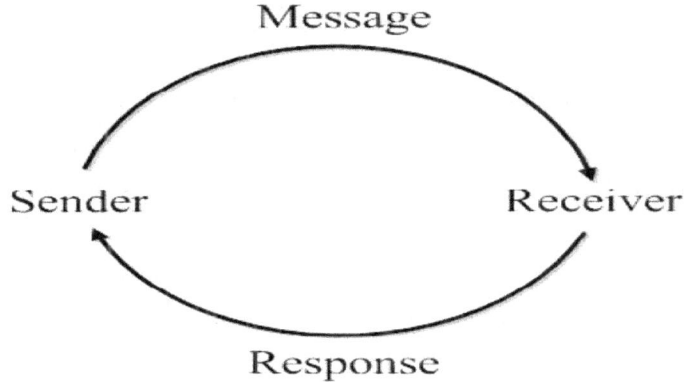

Learning Requires Basic Communication

An adequate structure in communicating subject matter creates an understandable message. A message is a well-defined unit of data from a reliable source that may be transferred to an individual or an audience using the acceptable methods of communication theory. Interactive exchange between sender and receiver should be considered stimulated interest in the subject not just conversational dialogue.

A basic difficulty in understanding the written or spoken word is not the vagueness of the subject matter, but the elusiveness of the author or speaker. This could be the reason English/European students read authors rather than subjects. The more one knows about the person responsible for the subject matter the easier it is to comprehend the message being conveyed. Knowing the orientation of a speaker and the background, philosophy, and purpose of the presentation increases acceptance and understanding gained from reading or listening.

Whether the sharing of subject matter is written or spoken, the observed structure of the paragraph and the essential elements must be followed. A paragraph must be one idea fully developed and (1) be founded on a topic sentence, (2) develop an evident progress of thought, (3) familiarize the receiver with the thought process by use of connective and transitional indications, and (4) make them aware of the place of the paragraph advances the message by some indication of function and value. This includes a transition to show how the paragraph idea logically connects with the next paragraph idea.

A developed manuscript or a lesson plan should follow the concept of emphasis by position or proportion. Words and phrases are emphasized by the position in the sentence. Sentences are emphasized by their position in the paragraph and paragraphs are emphasized by their position in the presentation. The most emphatic position is at the end of the sentence. The second most emphatic position is at the beginning. The same holds true for the sentences in a paragraph, paragraphs in a composition and chapters in a book.

Value is awarded to paragraphs and chapters by both position and proportion. Those last and first have position for emphasis and should be shorter. The others must be emphasized by size and proportion. Those paragraphs and chapters, which fall between the first and the last, must be given size according to their position. Paragraphs lost in the middle of a composition or chapters stuck in the middle should be larger in size and more carefully developed to maintain the attention of the reader and send the value-added message of the contents. The closer these elements are to the first or last position the less the size required for emphasis.

Here is the logical process. One thinks to formulate a central subject, then plans to arrange basic ideas (outline and paragraphs); next is the organization to present thoughts and facts in sentences to support the topic sentence of the paragraph. Paragraphs need a transition sentence to assist the clarity of how one idea is connected to the next idea. Always remember, a paragraph is one idea fully developed and so is a chapter.

Chapters need topic paragraphs and transitional paragraphs to show connection and organization of the central subject. A speech, book, article, lesson or report must be a string of pearls strung together with a recognizable theme.

The concept and construct of speaking and making learners *(disciples)* expressed in the Challenge of Jesus (Matthew 28:18,19) to followers clearly presents the teaching/learning process. The nature of the Greek language in Matthew 28:19 *"one teaches and the other learns or assimilates content into themselves."* Perhaps this is why most translators now see the word teach as meaning *"make disciples."* It is an *imperative* that actually commands one to teach others *(not only share subject matter, but to build a bond with the learner until they become attached to the teacher).* This connectedness is implicit in the words and is an *instructional command* for all leaders to be *"apt to teach."*

The basic verb form of "teach" is not found here in the Greek. Although the basic form means *to learn, but without any attachment to the teacher.* Could this be the reason the *(aorist imperative active)* form was used here? Must all teachers have an objective of bonding with students and making them into learners? To do this, presenters of subject matter must have a moral lifestyle that is transparent with a willingness to study and give a grounding to others. This is the essential element of the *"beyond"* pulpit, classroom or lecture hall. In reality, the presenter's uprightness and moral principles influence the whole process.

In the Gospel (John 15:15-17), there was a clear differentiation between a person obligated to be present for work and those who willingly embraced the opportunity to be involved. The Master Teacher called the latter "friends" suggesting a closer bond with the teacher and declared these were chosen to be fruitful and were to see that their fruit remained. The implication was that the force of things learned would remain with them all their lives. This is the power of gained knowledge and the camaraderie that good students and competent teachers develop with one another. It is a basic connectedness which some may call friendship or fellowship. This sounds comparable to *"making disciples."*

> *15. I no longer call you bond-slaves; because a bond-slave does not know what his Lord does: but you I have called you friends; for all things that I have heard of my Father I have made known to you. 16. You have not chosen me, but I have chosen you, and appointed you to go out and bring in fruit, and that your fruit should remain: and that you should obtain answers to your prayers to make them fruitful. 17. These things I command you, so that you may love one another.* (John 15:15-17 EDNT)

The basic elements of communication may be enhanced by the presenter's content and context, and the consent of the listener to concur with the presentation. Then there is the elusiveness of *semiotics* or the observed arrangement of words and language together that sends non-verbal signals which direct the listener away from the subject content. To reach a proper level of communications a speaker/writer must use the same language as the listener/reader, all encoding must be clear and not elusive, any preventable static or noise must be controlled whether heard or non-verbal. Some opportunity for feedback is essential to audience speaking their mind and the speaker learning from mistakes or omissions. Body language normally provides feedback to an experienced speaker.

Elements of non-verbal communications are present in the presentation of any homily, lesson, report, or speech. When it comes to feedback, the non-verbal aspects are important. Why? People have a street sense that makes speakers transparent and the average person can clearly see if someone cares or is just going through the motions. Sacred writings (Isaiah 3:9) suggest that even the appearance and facial expression can be read by an observer. The sincerity and genuine interest are primarily presented through personality, lifestyle and concern for others.

The treasure of knowledge is in earthen vessels and needs the light of understanding to shine before there is total acceptance. There must be reflected light from a Higher Power to assist in validating all presentation of subject matter. Something beyond the academic and professional qualifications of the presenter. Occasionally, when the opportunity presents itself "words" will have to be used to transfer information and to be sure the unspoken words of concern were heard and understood.

The conclusion of the matter: receivers must trust and verify. Individual in an audience should follow the example of the hearers at Berea: (Acts 17:11) *they were eager to receive the word and searched daily the scriptures to verify what was said.* It is assumed the Bereans verified the accuracy of the message by comparing what was said to the record in the Temple

Scroll. Likewise, serious listeners will check to validate sources of presented content. Learning is a two-way street. The communications channel must be cleared of static and distractions.

> *3. There will come a time when men will not tolerate healthy teaching; but following their own desires shall listen to many teachers because they are impatient to hear something to please and gratify their ears; 4. and they will stop listening to the truth and be turned aside to fictional tales. 5. You must be clear-headed in all things, endure hardships, declare the good news, fulfill your ministry.* (2 Timothy 4:3-8 EDNT)

While teaching seminary classes this concept was shared. Telling the class of would-be-pastors that who and what you are speaks so loudly that some will not listen to your spoken words. For example, a small child knows instinctively whether you love them. Even a stray dog can sense your fear or affection. And for sure you cannot fool the old folk because they have learned to hear with the ear of the **hear**t.

True stories that are stored in the speaker's mind, should be shared when they are relevant to the subject matter. Many good implications and non-verbal prompts to memory are indexed and retrieved for the audience in the memory of stories. Even though, serious or technical content may cause drowsiness, a good story can awaken the listener to action. A well told story is considered relational and usually creates a receptive mood in an audience. It is the peripheral role of stories which jog the memory of the listener and restores their interest in the speaker's presentation.

To communicate there must be a sender and a receiver; that is, someone to send a message and someone to receive the message. The sender must connect with the receiver and the receiver must show respect for the sender: respect means *"to look at and pay attention to" regardless of the venue or the presenter. The message must be adjusted to the present audience to be received.*

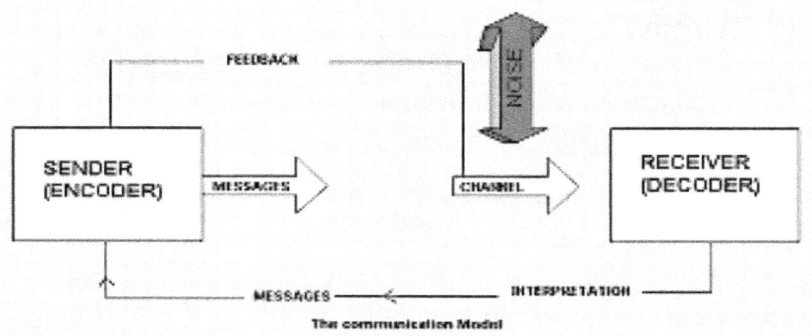

The communication Model

There are classic steps in messaging regardless of the subject, means of delivery or venue. The basic steps are:

1. **Connect** - there must be a connection that transmits subject matter between the messenger and the receiver.

2. **Communicate** - the messenger must recognize when the connection takes place and begin to share subject matter as information that is interesting and useful to engage the mind of the receiver.

3. **Concern** - the messenger must show interest and enable feedback that relate to the needs of the receiver.

4. **Comprehend** - the receiver must clearly accept the subject matter as relevant to their present

circumstance or as a summons to action, but if there is no analysis of content normally there will be conflict or no action.
5. **Consensus** - the messenger and receiver must bring their minds together and develop a harmony and solidarity on the message to complete the transaction.
6. **Conform** - the messenger and receiver must form an emotional bond and connect on an agreed pathway to assimilate and internalize the content of the message.
7. **Correspond** - the messenger must remain connected to the receiver in a manner that assures a continued and mutual benefit.

One must be studious in the disciplines of hermeneutics and homiletics to be an effective communicator. Preparing a manuscript or studying for a homily, research report, or teaching in a classroom, all must use the science of *hermeneutics* to *determine the root meaning of words*. Once the original intent of the words is determined, the speaker must find a way to render the meaning in common terms the audience would clearly understand. On the other hand, *homiletics* is the study of *preparing and delivering* a prepared manuscript.

The concern of *Hermeneutics* is the *rendering of the intent* of the original use of particular words presented in language that an intended audience would understand. Although *Homiletics* deals with the *preparation and delivery* of a homily, speech, message, discourse, lecture, lesson or report in any location, the message must be analyzed and perceived as enabling the receiver to reach desired goals and develop a sense of cohesiveness with others in order to produce action that meets current needs.

Situational analysis is a method used to interpret or analyze words or actions embedded in the context or linguistics of the source and the messenger. This analysis uses a form of dialogue as a means for understanding constructs beyond communication of words alone. It becomes an analysis from a "first-person" perspective based on intentionality of the messenger or the direction toward a particular purpose, objective or goal of the content and presentation.

Writing or speaking to impress others with personal knowledge will not produce learning. Write to be read and speak to be heard. Is your message to arouse interest, influence attitudes, solve problems, implement progress, or produce change? Keep in mind the three basic objectives in sharing a unit of subject matter: (1) to **inform,** (2) to **persuade,** and (3) to **interpret.** Choose the proper one. One may have to use the others to accomplish the chosen objective but concentrate on one reason.

Should your objective be to **inform,** state facts objectively and add subject data to the message. To do this, a judgment must be made as to the present knowledge the reader/listener may possess. When your objective is to **persuade**, attractive arguments and reasons should be used to push for a decision or a determined action. When you wish the reader/listener to make up their own mind, write to **interpret** by analyzing facts and sharing thoughts and positions on the subject.

Effective Subject Matter Transfer

- Effective transfer requires *advance preparation.*

- Effective transfer requires *analysis* of specific words in a source being studied to determine the intended meaning and determine the best way to transfer this in common language.
- Effective transfer requires *word-based analysis* a qualitative method to create structure to interpret, describe and communicate the characteristics of a specific unit of data.
- Effective transfer requires *historical analysis* to place the text within the original historical and cultura setting to better understand the meaning of words.
- Effective transfer requires *interpretative analysis* using the principles of interpretation to determire the significant value of a unit of information.
- Effective transfer requires *emphatic analysis* to relationships to better grasp the meaning.

Effective Learning

- Effective learning **requires** *attentive listening* as an informed participant with prior knowledge of the subject.
- Effective learning requires *supportive listening* to acquire both the specific and general meaning of the message.
- Effective learning requires an *emotional connection* with the speaker relative to the subject at hand.
- Effective learning requires *focused listening* with an uncluttered mind.

Academics have determined the basic language skills to be reading, listening, writing, and speaking. They are generally utilized in pairs: Reading and Listening and Writing and Speaking. When one is reading or listening, they are consuming a language; when one is writing or speaking, they are producing a language.

These skills are considered general competency to advance all learning while the development of specialized competency is required to advance in specific subjects.

My oldest son, Barton, is an accomplished and honored writer, first published at age 10. Decades later when he was serving as the General Editor of a Magazine, his first-grade teacher read an article and noted his name. Searching the Internet for other things written by Barton, and finding many, she sent a handwritten note and shared an unusual story about the first day she met him. It seems he tugged on her skirt as she passed his desk and asked, *"When do we learn to read?"* Intrigued by his eagerness she asked, *"Why do you ask, what is the hurry?"* Bart's reply, *"I am going to be a writer."* She wrote, *"I knew you were going to be a writer the first day in class. It was also my first day teaching school. I taught you to read and you are a writer."* God bless teachers who care about the learning and future career of their students and are willing to struggle to teach the general competency to assure their progress. In fact, those who teach advanced courses in Graduate School quickly learn that all adult students are but grown up children and still need the general competence plus the specialized competency to advance in academic excellence.

When an individual develops general competency to read, listen, write and speak, they are on their way to produce language and construct a long-term memory bank to which specific competency will be added as they mature and work at their chosen craft or profession. Writing produces language; it is hard work! As one learns the culture behind the language and tracked changes of words over time, and the basic theory of communications, the best way to improve writing skills is to write, rewrite, revise, review, reword, retype, etc. as time permits.

As one progresses in language skills, they build a vocabulary. A good unabridged dictionary provides root meanings and the tracked changes of words and original language and should become a writer's best friend. A computer thesaurus provides a choice of words, but no linguistic background needed by a writer. To remain relevant, a writer must constantly read refereed journals in their specialized field back for three years. After three years the best data is normally transferred to chapters in new books.

Develop a list of the best authors in your field of interest and buy their books. Never just read books, follow the European and English tradition of reading authors and subjects. Read authors who will teach you subject content as you learn their style of writing. Let the lazy writers read books, while you learn from the best subject authors. Should you fall into the American trap of reading titles instead of authors and subjects, you will find yourself with a stack of books with a celebrity's name on the cover but was written by some struggling writer trying to develop their talent and contacts. Beware of the books of celebrities, movie stars, luminaries, political figures or icons (they probably did not write a word of the book that displays their name on the cover). Perhaps we need an **Integrity Seal of Approval** that confirms the name on the cover wrote the book.

Communicate Strategy: First, use the K.I.S.S. (keep it short and simple) approach but have a deeper meaning beyond the words. Think broadly about the subject matter and consider the composition, education, cultural background as well as the social and economic factors of the audience. Be yourself; no pretense. Transparency is the key that unlocks acceptance provided the necessary investment of time and energy was made. Focus and structure come with effective communication.

Layout your emphasis in simple terms. Choose stories and vocabulary carefully. An effective speaker is able to bounce his subject-ball on the listener's court. Stories assist attention and recall of message content. They may forget the exact words, but they will remember the message of the stories you share. The Master Teacher constantly used stories to highlight a main point of His message. Also, listen for the unspoken words from the audience. Always adjust your voice volume to the audience and the size of words to their culture and education.

Instructional Guidance: Remember the three W's: What? So what? Now what? Present the subject (the what) in a guidance tone rather than an intellectual professional speaker. The "so what" provides a way to explain the value or importance of the content, and the "now what" is the real-life application of the essential meaning and benefit of the shared subject. The audience should feel they are competent to use what they learned presently and in the future.

Language Development: The essence of communication includes something beyond words; it includes both verbal and non-verbal skills. Reading, writing, speaking and listening are foundational skills of learning. Basic communication is more than words quickly put on paper or hastily spoken or any other impulsive means of transferring information; *for example,* the short form of texting. The style and speech of the verbal message s usually accompanied by non-verbal signals that indicate attitude, personality, and character: such as, writing style, stage presence, tone of voice vocabulary, stance, gestures, and facial expression are clues. Hall (1973) added time and space to the use of silent language and that these had less distortion than spoken language.

Developmental Maturity: Young writers and speakers should avoid the trap of passive reading; it is the pathway to poverty for many undeveloped writers and/or speechmakers. Passive reading fails to engage the content with an aroused spirit of inquiry. A strong foundation can produce a well-rounded writer and speaker in all fields of subject matter sharing. Developing language literacy through reading and listening can support a foundation for both composition and speech. The mastery of needed developmental skills and techniques may provide a head start in a crowded field. This comes though readings and listening skills: a form of developmental maturity.

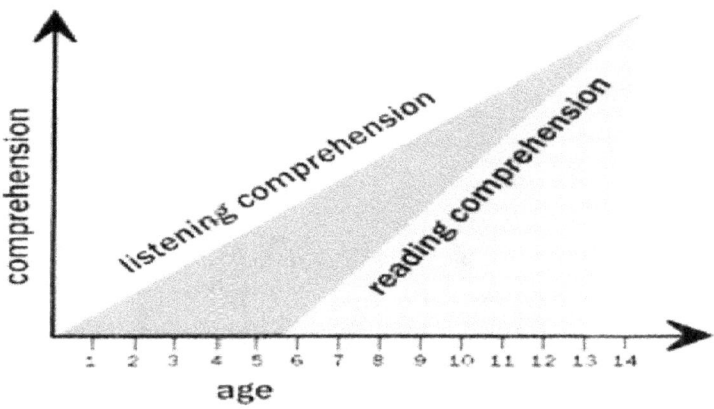

The actual meaning of words is in people, not dictionaries.

Chapter 10

Congregants and Education

*A congregant is a member
of a sacred gathering for worship
and religious instruction.*

When individuals come together in a faith-based assembly, they normally congregate for worship and guidance from spiritual leadership. This, and all communication, requires someone to send a message and someone to receive the message. The sender must connect with and appreciate the circumstance of the receiver and the receiver must show devotion and attribute value to both the message and the messenger. The meaning of words should be explained by the presenter or they will automatically be defined by the audience. In reality, the meaning of words is in people not dictionaries.

Regardless of the venue. the message source, or the presenter, the situation is similar. A cohort of students gather in a public classroom with good intentions expecting a value-added experience. An instructor taps into the instinctive desire to learn and guides the developmental process of education. Once the excitement of learning takes hold the student becomes ambitious and studies to improve competency by application of each tidbit of digested information to life.

The essence of education is to draw out or stretch the mind: this is teaching *par excellence.*

When an academic does social scientific research and arranges to report findings either by Journal, published book, or structured lecture, the audience is present because of prior knowledge and interest in the area of concern. The control of bias and the methodology utilized together with the statistical procedures used to test hypotheses and generate findings all inform the reliability and trustworthiness of the research. A Referred Journal article, a well-published book, or a quality presentation lecture to a receptive audience advances the field of knowledge. The reader or in person hearer all gain value added in a field of knowledge: this is the purpose of conducting and reporting research.

A communicator may share with an individual, small group, class, seminar, conference or a faith-based group. Provided worship is the primary emphasis, the homily must show the worth-ship of God in life and living and be *woven into the fabric of their faith.* (Hebrews 4:2 EDNT); provided the emphasis is directed to those needing a life-change, the message should be to put aside *all moral corruption and the abundance of worthless behavior and receive with a teachable spirit the firmly established word, which is able to make safe that spiritual part of you that determines all behavior.* (James 1:21 EDNT); should the message be for believers it should deal with the missional lifestyle expected of all who walk the straight and narrow path. A lifestyle that is truly faith-based will have a "missional" element that controls both attitude and action.

What is a missional attitude or predisposition to act? Such a commitment is not becoming a partaker of a divine nature, but a spiritual nature getting more control of the individual. The objective is a full dedication to become equipped for service to others at each and every opportunity. What is known about a missionary mindset is their willing to take the road less traveled and live and work outside their comfort zone. Each person met becomes an asset to advance their mission. A normal encounter may be initiated by *"Did God put you here to assist me or for me to assist you? Perhaps we can do something together for the good of mankind!"*

Most pioneer work is done outside the normal or safe channels, in the marketplace of ideas or the public square, along a rural road or on a jungle path. The work is difficult and is done on a limited budget with an awareness that each dollar spent must be replaced through deputation work to replace the funds already used. This further develops the spirit of adventure and discovery. This is an essential process for human progress.

No one adequately explained segregation and integration to the American public. Segregation was directed toward a racial group or class of people. A positive conclusion may not be reached beginning with a negative premise. Dr. King suggested a remedy by declaring *"one should be accepted based on their character rather than the color of their skin."* My paternal grandfather sat me down to an old piano and attempted to make a chord with only white keys, then with only black keys and finally with both black and white keys. The issue was harmony! He cautioned, *"accept each person as an individual and work with those who create harmony and the music of life will be better."*

The meaning of words is in people not dictionaries or documents. Words and phrases are defined by culture and context and have different meanings for different people. For example, part of the nation rejected a race of people, but accepted individuals based on behavior. Others claimed the moral high ground and accepted the whole race of people; then their words and actions did not completely match because they discriminated against individuals of the race they so boldly accepted. Such confusion was partly responsible for the Civil War, which was the subject of my senior thesis in college. The conclusion: Nothing was solved. When a relationship or interactive concern is over emphasized and/or misunderstood, the issue is confused and there is a setback in social progress.

Words can damage the cause for social justice. There must be comprehensive policy planning and the directing of large-scale operations to maneuver forces into an advantageous position prior to actual engagement for positive social change. Significant change cannot be affected over night; it takes time and patience to permit gradual constructive change in the social arena. This is done by interpreting the significance of words and phrases of various cultures and traditions into understandable language for all the people. This is the good path to social justice and positive social change.

At times words are used differently by various cultures and others get the wrong impression. For example, what the Russian leader said about democracy *"We will bury you,"* was grossly misunderstood. He was saying, Russia's idea of governance is new, democracy is a much older system, we will outlast you and be around at your demise. His statement was based on a Proverb in Russian culture about an old man and a young boy walking and musing about death, when the young man said, *"I will bury you."* This was a statement of courtesy. The young man felt that he would outlive the old man and would care for his final needs. It is amazing how a few words can be so drastically misunderstood. Differences should be minimized; commonalities must be accentuated. All progress comes through commonalities. Differences divide the people and confuse the issue. The highlight of any community effort toward social change should be the identification of common moral and human values that would advance the community toward tolerance and understanding across generational and cultural lines.

Attitude is expressed in the names given to identify events and circumstances. For example, during the Civil War, the North and South used different constructs to name battles: one used the nearest city or town and the other used the closest stream of water. Why? One saw the world as a structured township of people governed by others while the other a more rural society where water was essential to their crop growing and food production. This regional difference propagated two political mindsets: one which took the long view for the good of the nation and another who acted in ways necessary to win the next election.

One must correct the inferior assumptions before a superior proposal can be advanced. Segregation and integration appeared to have the same objectives, perhaps we should begin with a transparent assumption that segregation was a poor way to advance society. The legal bureaucratic language was applied incorrectly. Affirmative action must be accompanied by an affirmative attitude; i.e., a predisposition to act honestly and ethically toward others at all times. To accomplish this there must be a cooperative spirit between the sacred and the secular.

Faith-based declaration must work with the beneficial aspects of public education for the advancement of society. Individuals must be guided toward being a moral and productive member of society before they can be transformed into mystical citizens of a better world. The concept of separation on the basis of color that produced segregation was not good for America; neither were the processes of social integration productive. There must be a better way to mend American sensitive and create a moral way forward. Integration requires interaction at the intellectual and relational level. On Mar's Hill Paul suggested a pathway through the busy marketplace working with people who ask *"Can we learn more about this new teaching you speak about? You introduce strange terms and we want to know what they mean."* It is not affirmative action by organized government; it is affirmative attitude of the people who address the capabilities and commonalities of all mankind. There is only one race: the human race. Within God's will there is always a way forward! It may be the road less traveled, but to be victorious it must be taken.

> *24. The God who ordered the universe and all the things in it, the One being Lord of heaven and earth does not dwell in hand made shrines; 25. neither is He served by human hands, as*

though He needed something from man, seeing He gives to all life, breath, and all things; **26. and has made of one blood all nations of men who dwell on the earth, determined the history of nations and their territory;** *27. so they should search for God and hopefully find Him although He is not far from all of us. 28. For in Him we live and move, and have our being; he will judge the world* **with justice by the Man He has chosen and has provided assurance to mankind by standing Him up from among the dead.** (Acts 17:24-28 EDNT)

In social theory one learns that individuals change more rapidly than groups; groups faster than communities; and communities more easily than society. An affirmative attitude is needed to make a drastic difference, but legislation or groups of people are not the objective. Individuals are the persons who can change. Leadership is the ability to influence others to follow one toward stated objectives. It is influence that changes individuals, and changed individuals are able to influence group change. Then, small groups with an altered mindset can change the communities of which they are apart. Eventually, society will feel the force of gradual positive change. When it is gradual change over-time, social change will be accepted and even embraced. Most prefer instant change, but social change is sequential and incremental. Patience is required.

There is a social change timetable. For example, segregation in the United States began before the Constitution was written. Even that sacred document identified with the culture of the day. In the decade of the 1860's, the States fought a Civil War and President Lincoln signed the Emancipation Proclamation to free all slaves. In March 1870 the Fifteenth Amendment was ratified: *"The rights of citizens of the United States to vote shall not be denied or abridged by the United States or any State on account of race, color, or previous condition of servitude."* The following day, President Ulysses S. Grant signed the first Enforcement Act that substantially secured the voting rights of freedmen. One year later, Grant signed the Second Enforcement Act (1871) to protect black voting rights and targeted the activities of violent groups that resisted social progress.

Nearly five years later, President Grant signed the Civil Rights Act of 1875. This groundbreaking act prohibited segregation in various modes of public accommodations and transportation and discrimination in jury selection. President Grant's role in securing the full political equality of all Citizens regardless of color is unsurpassed in presidential history. Even after the popular will overwhelmingly turned against his efforts to protect the political and civil rights of former slaves, Grant refused to abandon his commitment to those for whose freedom he had fought.

After Grant left office, the federal government allowed the South to enter a new era of segregated disfranchisement. During this period, President Grant's efforts to protect the freedmen during Reconstruction were widely ridiculed and declared to be misguided. Such criticism, however, has crumbled in the face of history.

There has always been hopeful anticipation that change would come. About 100 years later in the 1960's, during a period of assassinations and civil disturbance, President Johnson signed more Civil Rights Legislation.

With patience and tolerance, perhaps by 2064, one hundred years later, the USA will develop a color-blind society and begin to function as a melting pot rather than a stew pot. This is hopeful anticipation based on the social theory timetable, but it should be remembered that discrimination and slavery did not begin with the Colonies or the Confederacy. It began in the evil hearts and cultural minds of people around the world who chose to look down on someone else because they perceived themselves to be superior. This discrimination built legal walls and social fences and created false human barriers to social progress in housing, education, the labor market and in the professions. Some remnants of discrimination remain that create roadblocks to social progress, educational and economical advance.

Some members of the minority have personally risen above the fray and been assisted over the wall and through the maze to a better life, but many individuals in minorities have been hindered in their personal and social progress. Some of the roadblocks have been within conservative politics, the religious community, inside community leadership, and sometimes within minority groups.

Some have said that Sunday morning is the most segregated hour of the week. Perhaps this is true, but is it by choice or tradition? When social integration works in education, housing, and the workplace, why is Sunday morning culturally divided? It is by choice based on cultural tradition and heritage.*

---

*One of my graduate students (Robert L. Allen, 1987) did a study to see if the progress of social integration would hinder the survival of Black Churches in the South. When three

> indices were compared: Social Integration Index, Black Church Participation Index, and Black Heritage Index, the level of social integration made no difference in church participation. Only the Black Heritage Index made a significant difference. The higher the Black heritage index the more apt one was to participate in an ethnic-based church. It was not segregation; it was cultural heritage that drew them to the worship and the music that fit their culture.

Is it possible for a minority to be integrated socially, economically, and educationally and still maintain some ethnic-based roots? It is obvious that most churches and all the denominations have a cultural control indicator. Scripture has been viewed through cultural glasses and the private interpretations differ from group to group. Consequently, universal truth became the exclusive domain of a particular religious authority and limited to a selected doctrinal or sectarian constituency. Various teachings and different doctrine were culturally interpreted but firmly and authoritatively proclaimed as the true and proper expression of the inspired sacred writings. While Judaism, the Roman Catholics, and members of Islam have differences, a unified message is presented to the world. The Protestant Christianity community accentuates differences as a badge of honor. Each group behaving as if they have found the *"Holy Grail" and have exclusive access to the "secrets" of faith and practice.*

Segregation and division in faith-based groups are facilitated within families and communities. Judaism has small internal differences, but the community maintains a unified identity. When individuals are identified as being Jewish, one immediately has an idea of their basic values. Although some differences exist among Roman Catholics, they manage to present a unified voice to the public. Other groups, such as Mormons, Jehovah

Witnesses, or Islam manage to overcome differences and present a common identity. This is not true of all communions. This complicates the integration of moral principles into society. *"Can two walk together except they agree on direction?"*

This is not a justification for religious segregation, but an explanation of how it happens by choice as part of their cultural expression and heritage. This will change over time, but it will change on its own, not by some external forces or even gentle public persuasion. The force for positive social change remains a personal choice and the affirmative attitude of individuals and groups. The trend in worship is moving away from a gathering of family and friends to a mindset which welcomes diversity.

There are common needs in all individuals as human development and education is approached. Education is to establish a knowledge base for life and career and define degrees of freedom and integration. Religion normally concerns moral behavior and a hopeful future. The separation of Church and State has pushed the growing gap between religion and education with great loss of the common kinship existing among human beings. There has been abject failure in the mature use of knowledge to prevent sectarianism in religion and segregation by class and socio-economic standing in society. The gap between the poor and the rich widens daily and generates more areas of concern.

Faith-based edification and general education together with advanced specialized competency has become categorized to the point of absurdity. The construct of sectarian separation in religion has become judgmental and counterproductive. The strict compartmentalization of education has created a branding and isolation of devotees. This writer firmly believes those who have only one point of view are wrong even if they are totally right. Unless one understands the perspective of another, there will be no teaching or learning. Mary T. Lathrap's 1895 poem about Indian tribes *"Judge Softly"* still speaks to this issue: *"Just walk a mile in his moccasins before you abuse, criticize and accuse. If just for one hour, you could find a way to see though his eyes, instead of your own..."*. To integrate, one must have at least two perspectives for contextualization and integration to occur where these overlap. Since all "truth" is beyond question, to cooperate one must respect the "truth" that others see and place their frame of reference in the context of that understanding. Without an integration of knowledge* there is no cooperation, no sharing, and no learning. Integration may then become the subject of scornful speech!

> ***Integration** – to make whole or new by adding or bringing together parts. The study of theology and/or philosophy creates one's identity and ideology. At the level of ideas and values, different individuals and divergent groups find common ground to effect positive social change in society.

The limited Bible content knowledge of churchgoers is well known among research scholars and has been confirmed over the years. In the 1980's and a follow-up study twenty years later, reported; *Persons who for 20 years had never or hardly ever attended church knew as much biblical content as regular churchgoers.* The class structure on Sunday had failed to meet the basic criteria for transferring data, information, and facts into congregational education. This speaks to weak public speaking from the pulpit and poor teaching in the classroom and few seem to care about fixing the problem.

Whether the group is private and faith-based or a cohort group in a public classroom instructed by a qualified teacher, the overlap of common knowledge creates common ground for positive cooperation and change.

The Sunday class structure failed to advance the common knowledge needed to support positive social change. Yet, when Bible History Programs were permitted in a public-school system based on pre and post-tests, considerable increase in bible content knowledge was validated. In a graduate course on how to integrate knowledge learned in education into operational value for Sunday school, a public-school teacher was asked how her church divided children for Sunday classes. Her answer was *"By age."* When pressed if that were the best way, her answer was *"No, I am a reading teacher, children should be tested to determine their reading level and placed with others at the same level, so they can learn."* This was a shock to several leaders in the class. However, it clearly explained that educated congregants, who understood the teaching and learning process, not only failed to intervene, but kept silent about the issue. The abject failure of Sunday classes to function adequately in educating the young was clear.

Sunday classes have no advance preparation or homework for the self-activity the educational process requires. Without the structured opportunity to prepare for and to use the information shared in class, there is little hope that permanent knowledge will result from the classroom experience. Education comes from the Latin, *e-duct,* and has the connotation of *drawing out or stretching out.* In fact, teachers become *learning leaders* involved in subject matter sharing with the intent of stretching students and weak learners out of ignorance into an understanding of how things work in the real world.

Records supported that public teachers could instruct effectively in biblical history and content when the Hamilton County Public Schools' Bible History Program* was initiated in Chattanooga, Tennessee. (1922) The stated purpose was to *enable students to become culturally literate and better equipped to thrive and contribute to a global world.* By default, the public schools are doing some of the work local churches should do; in some cases, doing it better. With elective courses and limited time in a public classroom, students increased their fact-based data on biblical history or content up to 127% assessed by pre and post-tests.

(See Appendix D or https://bibleintheschools.com/1.53/about)

Why does the church fail to accomplish similar results? The difference seems to be: *competent and consistent instruction in an adequate teaching and learning environment?* It is unfortunate that public schools could teach more effectively subject areas that most consider the purview of the church. Sadly six decades ago, Life Magazine's cover story stated, "Sunday School is the most wasted hour of the week." (2/11/1957) Tragically, the local Sunday class structure had become a small cohort gathering for fellowship and socializing without a significant learning experience. Sacred truth is not being woven into the fabric of their faith.

> *1. Let us be on guard, while the promise of entering His rest still holds; that none of you may be found to be delinquent and come up short. 2. The good news was proclaimed to us, as well as to them:* **but the word was not heard and therefore did not profit them, because it was not woven into the fabric of their faith when it was spoken.** *3. This rest is only to be attained by those who have* **learned to believe;** (Hebrews 4:1-3 EDNT)

Local leaders should remember that it took a well- educated Saul of Tarsus and the gentle pastor's heart of Barnabas, *"one whole year"* (365 days) of daily sessions of consistent teaching in one year to finish the task of concentrated and remedial work *before the word was woven into the fabric of their faith.* This was not the laissez-faire attitude without discipline or informed participation prevalent in Sunday classrooms today. A study/learning group requires a learning leader, coach or mentor to provide guidance for an informed discussion. Each Individual in the class must do advance study and willingly participate without the usual passiveness or commotion which fails to create a significant learning environment. Such behavior hinders both individual and collective growth in understanding and learning. Following the classic principles of teaching and learning will enhance the classroom experience and assist in the content being woven into the fabric of their faith and prevent bad behavior.

The end is worth the journey, but some are not willing to walk the pathway that prepares them for sharing or receiving subject matter to improve the application of learned information to real life circumstances. Years ago, the Sunday school stewpot reached the boiling point and most age groups lost interest in the social fellowship approach to Sunday classes. There was a need for a more structured educational program designed for age specific learning and scripturally based content in a Sunday classroom with a competent teacher.

C.A.F.E. ©
COMMUNITY AND FAMILY EDUCATION

(See Appendix C and D for operational details of C.A.F.E., A.I.M. and A.P.T.)

The objective and identity for this venture is **Community And Family Education (C.A.F.E.,).** The classrooms are set up informally in a café style. C.A.F.E. has a four-year curriculum cycle in a New Testament devotional study track on Sunday morning and a subject-based textbook track on Wednesday evening. There is also structured Accelerated Performance Tutorial (A.P.T.) sessions to assist public school students with remedial guidance in their most difficult subjects.

With the rapid decline in Sunday school attendance and a lack of general interest in religious study, the door of opportunity is standing ajar waiting for someone to walk through with a solution. The big question: where will we get qualified teachers and administrators?

In most churches there are sufficient mature members for the Bible study part, but qualified public school-type teachers were needed for A.P.T. subject-based remedial tutoring. In a personal interview/survey in one small Ohio city, forty-two (42) qualified individuals with a BA or BS who lived in the community were willing to offer their time and experience to do remedial tutoring in A.P.T. on Wednesday or by appointment with referrals from teachers, parents and the church.

Teachers were available. Yes, they represented the public-school system and may not be members of that local church. However, sufficient data were available that such qualified individuals could do special tutoring and even teach basic faith-based content and conduct better than some Sunday schools presently perform. It is appalling that some public-school teachers were more effective at teaching religious content than many educated churchgoers. (See Appendix D).

According to more recent polls by Gallup and Castelli: *"Americans revere the Bible, but do not read it. Consequently, they have become biblical illiterates."* One survey reported over 80 percent of Americans believed, *"God helps those who help themselves"* was a Bible verse. One poll discovered that about half of high school seniors believed *Sodom and Gomorrah were husband and wife.* Another group thought *the Sermon on the Mount was preached by Billy Graham.* This is a half century after Clyde Reid declared the American pulpit empty because no one was listening:

The pulpit today is empty in the sense that there is often no message heard, no results seen, and no power felt. The emptiness of which I speak is an absence of meaning, a lack of relevance, a communication failure. To be sure, this is a relative emptiness, not absolute, but it is emptiness, nevertheless. (Reid, *The Empty Pulpit*, 1967)

Based on Bonhoeffer's letters from prison, a similar condition existed in Germany at the end of WWII, a country that produced many of the academic and most of the theological textbooks studied by American clergy in seminary. Bonhoeffer wrote from prison shortly before his execution by the Gestapo, *"To think, the men perpetrating these atrocities sat in German churches for twenty years and it made no difference in their faith or behavior."* (essence of German translation). Bonhoeffer wrote at least seven (7) academic essays on Youth Work in an effort to prepare young Germans to lead the post-war church. This while America delayed intervention and concern for the slaughter in Europe, which created costly reconstruction and filled the minds and hearts with bitterness, greatly hindering moral and ethical leaders from guiding the world back to civility.

In one of my early books, *Why Churches Die* (1972) the growing gap between the pulpit and the pew expressed the reduced value of the pastor's homily, *"Proclamation is being downgraded even though the people are still willing to listen. Much of the fault is in the sender and not in the receiver. The problem is not to get the hungry to eat but provide sufficient food nutritious enough to meet the need."*

Sacred Scripture is Clear

25. But whosoever bows down to observe the complete prescriptive usage and the unrestrained opportunity to continue in the word and not become a forgetful hearer, but one who behaves the prescribed deeds, **this man shall by the blood be set apart for consecrated action.** *26. If any man among you seem to be devout, and restrains not his unnatural language, he deceives his own heart and his service to God is ineffective.* **27. Free from all that would dim the transparency in belief and conduct before God and the Father is this, to go see and relieve the orphans without a father's protection and the women lacking a husband in their distress, and to keep himself untainted with guilt.** (James 1:25-27 EDNT)

> Recommended reading: Green, **Remedial and Surrogate Parenting 2nd Ed. (2013) ISBN 978-1-9354344-81**—Children are a gift of God and a legacy of faith-based families; therefore, parenting skills are an essential aspect of human development. This work is guidance for remedial human development (0-20) for parents, teachers, and childcare workers.

Class structure in public schools or faith-based schools are best understood as regular study groups who meet to learn subject matter and make appropriate application of what was learned. Classroom and homework are more process than content; knowledge from class participation comes from listening and learning, and facts about a moral lifestyle that will improve learners, enhance families, and encourage active involvement in sharing what was learned with others, including both general and specific knowledge related to the venue. A class is of indefinite size but must be populated by regular attendees who are interested and willing to do prior study, participate in class, and do follow-up study assignments with both analysis and action.

All who prepare to teach or become an informed participant in class must find a quiet place to study. This requires persistence and concentrated effort. Mother was a schoolteacher and required me and my sister to be *"informed participants"* in public school and/or the Sunday classroom. With her full guidance, we began studying the next lesson on Sunday afternoon and on Wednesday she would ask one of us to teach the lesson to the family. Mother would evaluate and suggest ways to improve both our study and teaching techniques. Then on Saturday afternoon one of us would again teach the lesson and receive additional coaching. By Sunday in class we were willing and informed participants. This also strengthened performance in public school and improved grades and the personal mindset about education.

* * * * *

What is the value of reading a report, or perusing a published book, or attending a lecture series based on research findings?

> *First-hand knowledge from one who gave time, energy and resources to develop and execute a plan to find answers to stated questions, or discovered new pathways to solve old problems, is worthy of respect and the investment of time, energy and resources proportionate to the author's investment.*

Chapter 11

Research and Reporting

Research is personal discovery and a snapshot of findings may not be the first to reach the same conclusion; and may issue a false claim unintentionally.

Some may still believe Columbus discovered America! He did not live to be embarrassed, but with current technology any careless effort may be exposed even if it were unintentional.

Some years ago, my lecture on leadership at the Rolls Royce Plant in Derby, UK was followed by a tour of the plant. Several men were seen working inside a giant engine installing small fan-type blades on an engine for a multinational effort to build a super airplane. The project was having financial difficulties and seeking a bailout from various governments. Asking for one of the fan-blades to make a plaque: *"No one is too big to fail."* The guide said, *"The blades are made of secret material and could not be shared. If they were even slightly damaged, they could not be discarded but were melted down and the serial number recorded."*

Notwithstanding the security issues, the next morning my hotel key box contained a small package filled with cotton and wrapped inside was a broken fan-blade. The plaque was made and became a conversation piece in my office for years. It took years of research and labor to develop the material to make the almost indestructible fan-blades, but only the impulse of a visitor to break the code of behavior and place protected research essential to air travel in danger. The lesson learned in retrospect was clear: research is protected and must be acknowledged, appreciated and respected. To respect research is to *pay attention* to the report, the reporter, and the groundbreaking findings. To hear an author explain a book or a serious researcher relate what and why the research was done and learn the significant findings, is a rare privilege and should be respected and the added value honored.

My earliest memory of learning when some perspective or understanding came fresh to me, at the moment it was considered a "new discovery" made by me apart from all others. Of course, it was just the joy of learning from a good teacher. Later, when a significant insight came to me, it was a spiritual experience. Then when social scientific research methodology and statistics became a part of my studies, true personal discovery became possible. When valid research assumptions on a known problem were structured and hypothesized assertions were tested by the appropriate statistical procedures, the resulted findings were "new data" indeed. *Eureka* —a sudden triumphant discovery!

Sure, someone else could follow a similar research path and discover the same reality, but both the excitement of first discovery and then the realization that others would follow became head clearing events. Another awareness was the new knowledge came with the assistance of many instructors from past education and reading which prepared and paved the way forward. It was time to *"pay it forward."* Those who learn must also teach others!

Later, upon earning that the Greeks had two words for knowledge, my excitement was directed toward deeper study of semantics in linguistic changes in the meaning of words. From one perspective, the Greek *"gnosis"* knowledge came from *books and teachers,* but the other construct was *"epignoseos"* for full knowledge that came from *personal experience and/or investigative endeavors that produced first-hand experiential knowledge.* That one could learn educationally and spiritually through processing personal experience was encouraging.

When something was learned from an answered prayer or from using statistics to test hypotheses that produced valid findings, it was a fresh and new discovery. Learning through experiential discovery was exciting. Doing social research became a new way to generate useful special knowledge and experience the thrill of breakthrough discovery. The reporting and sharing of research findings became a passion: this being my 56th book to share past experience and learning. Hopefully, it will be part of my academic legacy.

Serious research requires advance training as well as a prior knowledge of the subject matter. An academic may do continuing research in a field of expertise to answer frequently asked questions, to find possible answers to pressing problems, or add to the available data in a particular aspect of a field by creating a new syllabus or textbook.

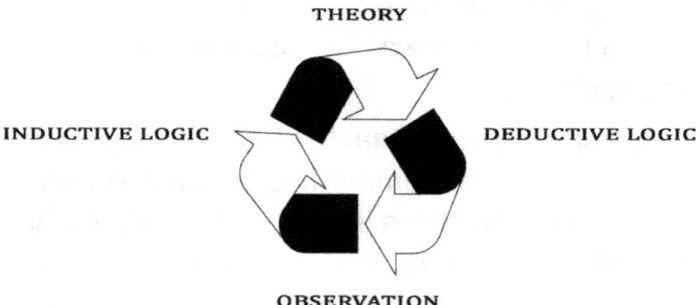

The Wheel of Research
Hunch + Assumptions + Assertions + Objectives + Lit Review + Research Hypotheses + Statistical Hypotheses + Observations + Conclusions + Generalizations

An early step in social research begins with a foundation in education and significant reading in an academic field. To do research one must have prior knowledge of the subject to be studied in order to ask the proper questions and make reasonable assumptions. Prior knowledge creates a *hunch* about possible answers to important questions or probable solutions to a present problem.

Assumptions about a question or problem are the rungs on the research ladder which must be constructed to reach and cross the threshold to reliable and valid findings; then based on prior knowledge *assertions* may be made about the areas of concern relative to the problem. These *assertions* will become *objectives* for the research and guidepost for the journey of developing a comprehensive *literature review.*

In social scientific research, an *exhaustive* review of literature is not required; however, it must be tied to the objectives/hypotheses of the planned research. Although not exhaustive as in *qualitative* studies, *quantitative* research must be *comprehensive* with a date specific end.

A *comprehensive review* is a major step forward dealing with relevant material both print and electronic which equips the researcher to finalize *hypotheses:* some preliminary hypotheses, based on the review, may be discarded because findings in the area are already reported. Also, the review may discover a new concept or construct which suggests an additional area of development which would permit an additional hypothesis that was not included in the original assumptions-assertions-objective process. *Quantitative* research is supported by the use of statistics, while *qualitative* studies use Boolean logic to interpret a proposition to be true or false.

The *literature review* for quantitative research is comprehensive but not exhaustive; it deals only with assumptions and objectives of the research to enable the development of hypotheses. The work of others in the field must be adequately considered, remembered, respected, and documented in the process of structuring a research strategy to develop *testable hypotheses.*

Once research hypotheses are changed to statistical or null form, a giant step has been taken in determining the *methodology* to be used and the *statistical procedures* that will be required to test each hypothesis in the *statistical* or *null form of no difference.* This transformation is necessary for *statistical analysis* to support or reject Null Hypothesis of no difference and *to control the bias* of the researcher.

What is the value of reading a report, perusing a published book, or attending a lecture series based on research findings? An appreciation for and a knowledge of the painstaking process of research is *value added* to the findings. Exposure to research findings would benefit anyone desiring to gain usable information in a field. First-hand knowledge from one who gave time, energy and resources to develop and execute a plan to find answers to stated questions or discovered new pathways to solve old problems is worthy of respect and the investment of time, energy and resources proportionate to the author's investment.

Why is this important? The author of a report on research results invested an almost unfathomable amount of time in conception, advance reading of literature, designing a scientifically approved structure, gathering and analyzing data and writing a report in an academic format acceptable to other academics. To gain proportional value, the reader or listener must be an informed participant in the process with prior knowledge of the area of concern with the same spirit of inquiry and the desire to apply the findings in a relevant application.

This is based on the signs in algebra: < *less than;* = *equal to;* > *more than.* In a mathematic equation the data on both sides of the "equal" sign must be equal or balanced in comparison. Thus, if the reader or listener makes little or no effort to prepare in advance and is not an informed participant, there will be little understanding and value from exposure to research findings.

Seriously studying a professional journal article on recent research examined by an editorial board, or critically evaluating a quality book, eagerly attending an author's lecture on research findings, or welcoming the opportunity to register for a series of lectures developed from social scientific research by an academic endorsed by a learned society, would be profitable for anyone desiring to gain usable knowledge. However, those who wish to profit from exposure to the results of social research must be adequately prepared to both accept and understand the facts in the report. A willingness to learn with the intent of application in a practical laboratory is the best path to profitable use of what is learned from the research of others.

Although developing the ability to comprehend and structure valid and reliable first-hand research is an asset to any career, critical exposure to the quality exploration of others saves time and effort in adding to the knowledge base in a field of study. Such participation may answer questions, provide possible solutions to a social problem, or contribute to specialized knowledge in a field of study. Everyone exposed to the findings of quality social scientific research will gain usable data, information, or facts to assist with answering questions or solve problems. It is time and effort well spent listening and learning directly from a knowledgeable scholar with validated skills and integrity.

Only a few have sufficient general knowledge to write an essay, a journal article, or a book without prior study and research. Certainly, one would not attempt to develop an academic syllabus, author a textbook or write a thesis or a dissertation without an adequate comprehensive reading of relevant literature in the area of concern. A literature review must be comprehensive, but not necessarily exhaustive. These questions should be considered as one considers relevant literature with substantial effort:

1. What is already known about the subject?
2. What are the gaps in the knowledge of the subject?
3. What areas of further study have been identified by other authors?
4. Who are the significant authors in this area?
5. Is there consensus among the primary authors on the subject?
6. What aspects of the subject have generated debate?
7. What methods or problems were identified in the reported research?
8. What is the most productive methodology for the review?
9. What is the current status of research on the subject?
10. What sources of information or data were identified that might be useful in the new research?

Social research is not complicated; it is sophisticated. Social scientific research is an invention of humans and has been developed over time. This refinement causes complexity and specialized knowledge to be required to simplify the methods and the process. Once those methods and procedures are understood the methodology no longer appears to be complicated. A *logical trichotomy* in the research process is clear:

1. The process of developing a plan or proposal
2. The gathering and analysis of data
3. The report that shows research findings

The proposal is a "we –process." There are regulations and procedures which must be followed. A comprehensive review of relevant literature is necessary to place the research problem in the context of the completed research of others. The proposal process is normally guided by mentors or advisors. This makes the research proposal a "we project." Notwithstanding, the "we-ness" of bouncing the ball on another's court, for proposal approval, the academic research process, that of gathering and analyzing data, testing hypotheses, and reporting findings is a most "personal process." The actual research is a "me" thing!

Research is a planned and detailed process. Hunches, expectations, and assumptions should be developed early. A plan of action should be followed by which another independent researcher using the same plan would achieve similar results. Such plans should include objectives, methods, and procedures, the significance of the research, pertinent literature review such as previous research that relates to the problem, descriptions of the results obtained by the other related research, and other supporting information. Methods of research tend to vary from discipline to discipline, but research generally follows similar basic comprehensive plans.

A proposal is basically a means of introducing a researchable idea, either to academia or a funding source. The actual format of research is normally specified by an academic program, a discipline, or a corporate research entity. The proposal for a theoretical study employing *qualitative* methods that emphasize intuitive induction, description, the study of environments, attitudes, and perceptions should contain a specific statement of approach, methodology and extensive literature review, but no testable hypotheses. Research that employs **quantitative** methods would require a more structured proposal, presenting a specific focus supported by a literature review and testable hypotheses. Such a proposal should include a design for the research with descriptions of sampling procedures, the instrument to be used in data gathering and data analysis procedures.

Scientific research is a freeze-frame snapshot of a fixed time period. Perhaps it is this characteristic that fixed the earliest inquiries on questions of origin and existence. Literally, the derived meaning suggests two fundamental characteristics: (1) diligence of inquiry and (2) a temporal relationship only to the present and past, although a basic reason may be to predict and control the future.

The meaning of the word research is *"to seek again or investigate exhaustively."* Presently, this word is used to describe a wide range of human inquiry and in the estimation of this author should never be used carelessly or inaccurately without a grasp of the process. A diligent searching again of the past reveals that existence, moving over time, has order, patterns, and sequences. The discovery of relationships that persisted over time made it possible to seek answers to questions about the future. Predictive instruments, such as calendars, were based on observed recurring patterns of the past. This is a scientific age and many who hear the word "research" assume the speaker or writer has done exhaustive investigation.

Could a solution of the problem advance knowledge and contribute to my field of study? Can the results be adequately generalized to the population studied? Will the findings be of practical value? Has the literature review placed the problem in the context of existing research? Will the research replicate another study? If so, was the subject extended beyond previous limits? Has the subject been sufficiently delimited to assure an exhaustive study yet important enough to support further study? Will the data gathered from a sample of the population be reliable and the conclusions valid? Will the methods used be sufficiently rigid, and the controls adequate to cause others to trust the conclusions?

All progress and positive social change start with some dissatisfaction or frustration generated by mundane work and the basic fear of change. Lewin's Force field theory was an influential development for analysis in the field of social science. It provided a framework for understanding the positive and negative factors that influenced change. It considers driving forces and restraining forces that either produce or inhibit change. The theory, developed by Kurt Lewin, was a significant contribution to the fields of social science, psychology, social psychology, organizational development, process management, and change theory. Hopefully, it can be used to remove the fears in ministry and education about using social research to improve the quality of preparation and delivery.

Complexity is a major obstacle to scientific investigation. Consequently, simplification methods must be employed. Modern scientific research widely uses statistical inference to overcome the complexity of measuring all objects of interest. Generally, statistical inference is based on a combination of measurement theory and involves procedures of hypothesis testing.

These three important elements of scientific research are related and, in fact, integrated. Finally, hypothesis testing is achieved within the confines of controlled observation by proper research design. Here it is important to realize that all "scientific studies" are not necessarily good science.

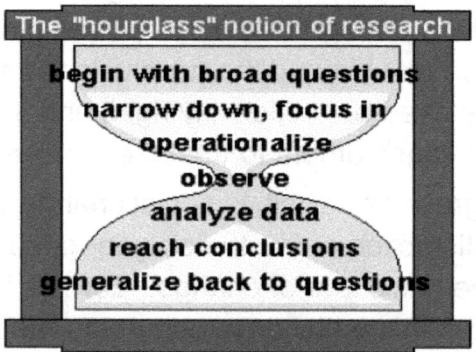

Common Concerns of Social Research

Ockham's Reasoning: The 14th century English logician and Franciscan friar, William of Ockham, established benchmark in reasoning about the explanation of any unexplained incident or experience. He suggested the best explanation or solution would be based on as few assumptions as possible, eliminating those that make no difference in the observable predictions of the explanatory hypothesis or theory. The principle is often expressed in Latin as the *lex parsimoniae* -*"law of parsimony"* or *"law of succinctness:"* *"entia non sunt multiplicands praeter necessitate,"* roughly translated as *"entities must not be multiplied beyond necessity."*

Rule of Thumb: This is often paraphrased as *"All other things being equal, the simplest solution is the best."* In other words, when multiple competing theories are equal in other respects, Ockham recommended selecting the construct that introduces the fewest assumptions and suggests the fewest entities. It is more often taken today as an exploratory guideline or *rule of thumb based on experience or practice* that advises common sense, economy, prudence, or simplicity, especially in the scientific speculation. In this sense Ockham's Razor is useful in the area of social research. It also suggests that social scientific research is best left to individuals prepared by specialized training rather than the guessing or trial and error of amateurs. The rest of us should read their books, listen to their research findings, and perhaps enroll in a Lecture Series by a learned academic.

All reliable research is structured to provide transparency in the process of gathering and analyzing data. Those who would trust the research findings must see that standard methodology and design were employed and a feasible strategy developed based on the complexity of the research problem. Research literature offers standard and nonstandard design scenarios for research. Some are too preliminary for testing hypotheses and others too expensive and time consuming to be practical. Still others require the security of a university-type laboratory. Most social research will be lodged in organisms, groups, communities, and organizations. And will deal primarily with societal issues of *production, protection and preserving of individuals* in the context of these basic institutions. This requires a great deal of critical thinking and discovery utilizing the technical process of social scientific research.

Being able to distinguish between a statement of fact, opinion or an inference is an important contribution to reading, writing, speaking and listening.

Chapter 12

Critical Thinking and Discovery

It is best to correct the substandard before attempting to construct the exceptional.

Critical thinking is central to all attempts to advance society, particularly in the discovery of new information in the area of problem solving. Whether a research report, instruction in a classroom, or the approach to delivering a homily, all are improved by critical thinking, serious study, advanced preparation and a dose of inspiration and perseverance. My personal career has been a ministry through education: teaching, developing educational programs, and leading non-profit sociological integration of religion and society efforts. These endeavors were advanced by the universal principles of critical thinking.

Using critical thinking to objectively examine and evaluate issues to make a decision is both foundational and functional to any endeavor. Critical thinking is an important aspect of all advance study in order to carefully acquire and interpret data and reach a valid conclusion to make proper application of findings. It is best to correct the substandard before attempting to construct the exceptional. One must remember that mistakes may happen due to personal bias, even when the methods of logical inquiry and reasoning are used. The identification and control of bias is part of the integrity of the social research process.

Critical thinking can assist in identifying the preconceived notions that invalidate research findings and sidetrack the move toward positive social change. Hypotheses are tested in null form to protect the research from personal bias and to discover the difference or no difference in variables and to support or not support the initial assumption and assertions about the problem. Diagnostic assessment is related to crucial areas of concern within the problem area.

Such a process is a careful and deliberate process as to acceptance or rejection of a conclusion and the degree of confidence with which the judgment is accepted. Fundamental flaws and errors in thinking and methodology may be detected through a situational-type analysis by studying both the internal and external aspects of the problem environment: this is critical thinking.

Problem solving and critical thinking are connected at essential points: identifying the problem, constructing clear assumptions, determining methods, developing procedures, collecting and analyzing data, in order to make reliable and valid conclusions based on supported assumptions. Critical thinking employs not only logic but broad academic criteria and appropriate theoretical constructs for understanding the problem, the gathered data, and the methods of analysis that unearth the findings. The questions of reliability and validity of data and generalizability of findings must be answered. One may not make general statements and/or application of findings beyond the sample or population investigated.

Taking the broad view of findings rather than specific application normally invalidates the conclusions.

Thinking about a problematic issue normally renders a question neutral and requires reasoning which may express negative consequences and must be put aside and replaced with the objectively based tools of critical thinking. Such thinking requires knowledge of logical inquiry and the reasonable ability to apply these skills to the problem at hand. (Glaser, 1941) This is a persistent process that examines both the fact-based thinking and the process which produced the conclusions. Critical thinking requires the ability to recognize unrelated expectations and known patterns of relationships between correct thinking and assumptions. The use of appropriate thinking and language are essential to navigate this extensive process and breakthrough to reliable findings.

Diagnostic thinking presupposes rigorous standards in assumptions about problem solving and a-best-guess judgment about antecedent causes or influences that impact the present situation. Analytical thinking is a regimented process that assists in conceptualizing a problem, framing operational methods, controlling the structured process, gathering reliable data and comparing variables with grounded reasoning that leads to a valid conclusion. It involves assessment of elements of structures and essential aspects of the solution design and procedures used to gather and analyze data. Critical thinking habitually uses competence in logic and proficiency in approaching problem solving. The soundness of the process and the control of bias brings integrity to the findings and strengthens the acceptance of conclusive answers or applications.

Critical thinking is essential in social scientific research; it is a process that assists with the control of bias. Flawed thinking can cause havoc to many aspects of life. Critical thinking avoids a one-dimensional view of difficult issues and produces a self-evaluation that exemplifies the principles illustrated in Plato's account of the trial and death of Socrates: namely, that *the unexamined is not worthy of existence.* In other words, each step in problem solving deserves inspection and analysis to be worthy of acceptance. This self-activated action of imposing intellectual standards on the thinking process must be systematically cultivated and utilized in the social professions. When adequately used, critical thinking tools can build confidence and assure the integrity of those working with individuals, cohorts, social groups and organizations to advance their findings.

Paraphrasing Glaser's influential study on analytical thinking and making an application to speaking, teaching, and research reporting would identify critical thinking in three areas. There must be an objective attitude about the problem and subjects within the range of personal experience. Knowledge of fact-finding methods, including reading, writing, speaking and listening, can produced systematic thinking about problem solving. Finally, the application of appropriate and adequate proficiency with suitable methodology is essential to social scientific investigation. (Glaser, 1941)

Applying critical thinking to social scientific methodology requires one to think diagnostically in the research process. The close relationship to critical thinking tools and research methodology is easily observed. The skills required in social research are matched in the process of analytically thinking about the issue; or perhaps a better wording would be *evaluative thinking* which determines the significance, worth, or condition of use by careful appraisal and study.

ED = T P O

WRRRRRR / RRR

T

Effective Delivery= Think – Plan –Organize (TPO)

Write – read, revise, rewrite, revise, revise / revise

[Time]

Follow the TPO formula (think, plan, organize) of rhetoric before you compose a proposal. This plan is based on aspects of Greco-Roman rhetoric: *invention, disposition, and elocution (delivery)*. Aristotle identified the first three steps in the rhetorical process as invention, arrangement, and style of delivery, but he added three aspects to bring credibility to the author: *ethos, pathos, and logos*. The Roman philosopher, Cicero, added style and memory to the process.

Ethos is a demonstration of *what* the author knows of the subject that *influences* the reader to accept the author's work as believable. *Pathos* is a construct relative to the author's way of *presenting a topic* that evokes response in the receiver. *Logos* has to do with *logical reasoning and objectivity in constructing* a document for delivery. Although these concepts are from the classical period centuries ago, they remain trusted guideposts for investigators, creative thinkers, and all who deal with *composition* intended to persuade. The meaning of com *"together with"* and position is simply *"together with" position, place, status or rank.* Everything has a place or a position of emphasis either by position or proportion, in the development and presentation of a written or spoken effort to convey subject matter.

A hypothesis is not constructed until the critical thinking process is completed and a theoretical construction for research is made. First, there will be a *"hunch"* about the relationship of the existing problem to possible antecedent influences on the issue. The next step is using the interrogatives: *who, what, why, how, when, etc.* This will provide basic *assumptions* about preconditions that influenced the creation of the present problem.

All academically prepared individuals developed critical evaluation techniques to reach their present level of achievement; these skills, however, are not always functional in speaking and teaching. Both require similar steps: problem identification and basic assumptions, formulation of design, operational definitions, purpose/problem statement, scope and limitations, methodology and data analysis procedures, that include engaging the data for findings which did not cluster around assumptions or serendipitous findings that could enhance the contribution to the field. This is a learned process which enables further research.

Critical thinking relates to the social professions and is a scholarly behavior and a means of correct thinking in the pursuit of relevant and reliable information about solving particular issues. A critical thinker can normally ask appropriate questions, gather relevant facts, efficiently and creatively sort through data, reason objectively and decisively from the information at hand, and process the data accurately in a rigorous manner and make good decisions. In other words, critical thinking involves serious investigation and practice makes the process better, not necessarily perfect.

All research findings are based on the population studied and a snapshot in data gathered and evaluated at a particular time and place. For example, scientific "truth" is relative: on a hillside in Greece a man counted 4,000 stars, but later a telescope was used, and a man counted 20,000 stars, then a larger telescope, etc., etc... scientific facts change with more observations and snapshots.

The social research process does not seek truth or proof, only support for previous assumptions. The hard sciences seek evidence of an antecedent cause or the "why," while social research seeks answers to the question of "how" by asking *what, when, where,* how long and by whom to judge the ongoing impact on others. With these interrogatives, answers are determined as to *why* something happened. For example, an autopsy determines *how* the person died and then they know *why* and may construct procedures to prevent future deaths from the same cause or malfunction. Social scientific research informs both the present and the future.

Since problem solving is critical thinking, it is reasonable to conclude that the process of problem solving is connected to the process of reasoning. Being able to distinguish between a statement of fact, opinion or an inference is an important contribution to reading, writing, speaking and listening. An excellent method to obtain relevant and reliable information about a given subject and know what can be supported by analysis of language and legitimately derived from language and documented facts is crucial to writing and speaking.

Exposition, instruction, and research findings in subject matter sharing revealed there were no significant differences in speaking whether from a pulpit, in a classroom or a lecture hall. The objectives were clear; accurate and detailed communication. The intent and function of sharing subject matter by speaker and location may be the only definable differences together with many more similarities. Conveying subject matter requires advance preparation, comprehensive knowledge of the subject, and a focus on the venue and the audience.

ABOUT THE AUTHOR

Hollis L. Green, ThD, PhD, DLitt, is a Clergy-Educator with public relations and business credentials and doctorates in theology, philosophy, and education. A  Distinguished Professor of Education and Social Change at the graduate level for over four decades, Dr. Green is a Diplomate in the Oxford Society of Scholars, and author of 50+ books and numerous articles. He served six years as a member of the U.S. Senate Business Advisory Board and maintained certified membership in several public relations societies (RPRC, PRSA, and IPRC). He served pastorates in five states, a Military Chaplain during the Vietnam era, a denominational official for 18 years, and traveled in ministry and lectured in over 100 countries.

Dr. Green was the founder (1974) A.I.D. Ltd., Associated Institutional Developers, Ltd. (an international Public Relations and Corporate Consultant Company). He was Vice-President (1974-1979) of Luther Rice Seminary (www.lru.edu) and became the founding President (1981) and Chancellor (1991-2008) of Oxford Graduate School, [www.ogs.edu]. As part of a global outreach, Dr. Green founded (2002) OASIS UNIVERSITY in Trinidad, West Indies [www.

oasisgradedu.org] where he continues to serve as a Professor of Education and Social Change and Chancellor. In 2004, he assisted in establishing Greenleaf Educational Foundation in Colorado to advance higher education.

    In addition to other endeavors, Dr. Green launched Global Educational Advance, Inc. and GlobalEdAdvance Press (2007) [www.gea-books.com] to advance higher education and positive social change through publishing, curriculum advance, library/learning resources, improved instruction, and global book distribution. His books and assisting authors in publishing are a logical outgrowth of a sixty-year ministry through education. He serves Global as Corporate Chair and Co-publisher with his sons, Barton and Brian. Dr. Green continues to travel, speak, teach, write books and work with authors in publishing quality creative work.

Afterword

The Reverend Dr. John Buuck
President Emeritus: Concordia University—Wisconsin
Founder: Wisconsin International University
[Estonia, Ukraine, Ghana, and Liberia in process]

Dr. Green once again demonstrates his gifts as a scholar and an author. The book, *Beyond Pulpit, Classroom and Lecture Hall,* is about preachers, teachers, and academic scholars. While these disciplines appear significantly different, Dr. Green elaborates on what all three have in common. Each discipline requires qualified professionals using appropriate language that is understood by the listener using basic communications structure.

The author is experienced in the disciplines covered in the book: preaching, teaching, and research reporting. He has been widely acclaimed internationally in each discipline as an effective speaker. In this book, he is sharing his vast knowledge of delivery and communication skills in different venues. Dr. Green is patient and persuasive in guiding individuals in improving skills in conveying subject matter regardless of the time and place. He gracefully and artistically, with integrity, provides examples of experiences in public speaking in different situations.

While it is understood that each profession must have knowledge of their subject matter, some effect the listener differently. Personality, enthusiasm, confidence, passion, authenticity, preparation and integrity are attributes of a good speaker. Every speaker with guidance and practice can improve on these attributes.

I highly recommend this book!

Appendices A-D
&
Bibliography

# APPENDIX A — SURVEY FORM

Mark Preaching, Teaching or Both

Do not view the Results of Survey until after completing the form

Mark [x] words associated with Preaching Teaching Both

- advising   [.]   [.]   [.]
- admonishing   [.]   [.]   [.]
- advocating   [.]   [.]   [.]
- applying   [.]   [.]   [.]
- caring   [.]   [.]   [.]
- clarifying   [.]   [.]   [.]
- coaching   [.]   [.]   [.]
- communicating   [.]   [.]   [.]
- confronting   [.]   [.]   [.]
- concluding   [.]   [.]   [.]
- counseling   [.]   [.]   [.]
- correcting   [.]   [.]   [.]
- edifying   [.]   [.]   [.]
- encouraging   [.]   [.]   [.]
- evangelizing   [.]   [.]   [.]
- exhorting   [.]   [.]   [.]
- explaining   [.]   [.]   [.]
- exposition   [.]   [.]   [.]
- expounding   [.]   [.]   [.]
- instructing   [.]   [.]   [.]

APPENDIX A — SURVEY 233

<u>Mark Preaching, Teaching or Both</u>

Do not view the Results of Survey until after completing the form

Mark [x] words associated with   Preaching   Teaching   Both

- illustrating [.] [.] [.]
- lecturing [.] [.] [.]
- mentoring [.] [.] [.]
- moralizing [.] [.] [.]
- motivating [.] [.] [.]
- persuading [.] [.] [.]
- proclaiming [.] [.] [.]
- reading [.] [.] [.]
- sharing [.] [.] [.]
- speaking [.] [.] [ ]
- storytelling [.] [.] [ ]
- training [.] [.] [.]
- tutoring [.] [.] [.]
- writing [.] [.] [.]

Preaching [.]

Teaching [.]

Both [.]

Copy, complete and email form to:
greenoxon2@gmail.com

Results of Survey

Since everyone seemed to see little difference in preaching and teaching, the results were predictable: only 4 were marked for teaching: [advising, advocating, mentoring and tutoring] and 6 scored exclusively for preaching: [confronting, evangelizing, exhorting, expounding, illustrating, and proclaiming] while the balance of 26 terms were scored for both preaching and teaching: [admonishing, applying, caring, clarifying, coaching, communicating, concluding, confronting, correcting, counseling, edifying, encouraging, explaining, exposition, instructing, lecturing, listening, moralizing, motivating, persuading, reading, sharing, speaking, storytelling, training, and writing.] This supports the understanding that much sameness exists in the two functions. Difference seems to relate to subject, assignment, venue and the personality and intent of the speaker.

APPENDIX A — SURVEY 235

SUMMARY REPORT

Preaching - Teaching - or Both

Mark [x] words associated with	Preaching	Teaching	Both
• advising	[.]	[. x]	[ ]
• admonishing	[.]	[.]	[x]
• advocating	[.]	[.x]	[.]
• applying	[.]	[.]	[.x]
• caring	[.]	[.]	[.x]
• clarifying	[.]	[.]	[.x]
• coaching	[.]	[.]	[.x]
• comforting	[.]	[.]	[.x]
• communicating	[.]	[.]	[.x]
• confronting	[. x]	[.]	[.]
• concluding	[.]	[.]	[.x]
• counseling	[.]	[.]	[.x]
• correcting	[.]	[.]	[.x]
• edifying	[.]	[.]	[.x]
• encouraging	[.]	[.]	[.x]
• evangelizing	[.x]	[.]	[.]
• exhorting	[.x]	[.]	[.]
• explaining	[.]	[.]	[.x]
• exposition	[.]	[.]	[.x]
• expounding	[.x]	[.]	[.]
• instructing	[.]	[.]	[.x]

- illustrating [.x] [.] [.]
- lecturing [.] [.] [.x]
- mentoring [.] [.x] [.]
- moralizing [.] [.] [.x]
- motivating [.] [.] [.x]
- persuading [.] [.] [.x]
- proclaiming [.x] [.] [.]
- reading [.] [.] [.x]
- sharing [.] [.] [.x]
- speaking [.] [.] [.x]
- storytelling [.] [.] [.x]
- training [.] [.] [.x]
- tutoring [.] [.x] [.]
- writing [.] [.] [.x]

===

Preaching [.6];   Teaching [.4]   Both [26]

APPENDIX B

Other Books by the Author

To understand the problems of faith-based entities and advance delivery systems for graduate education, extensive research was done during the past two decades. Meanwhile, his schedule was filled with academic administration, teaching, research and writing, but colleagues and friends have encouraged sequels to his best-known works. In the post-retirement years, Dr. Green followed that prompt and produced twenty (20+) books plus ten Children's Novellas.

(See www.gea-books.com.bookstore**)**
or anywhere good books are sold.

- **Why Churches Die.** (2007) ISBN 978-1-9796019-03 A fresh assessment of congregational vitality to determine thirty-five reasons why faith-based congregations were losing their pristine power of outreach.
- **Interpreting an Author's Words.** (2008) ISBN 978-0980-164-74—Define both formal and informal study and writing skills by understanding how to clearly interpret the spoken and written words of others.
- **Titanic Lesson.** (2008) ISBN 978-0-9796019-6-5 -- An answer to the question: "Do historic realities predict problems for a growing faith-based group?
- **Sympathetic Leadership Cybernetics.** (2010) ISBN 978-1-9354345-28 – This work attempts to clarify management and leadership in the context of organizational and institutional functionality and charts a course for organizations to serve the needs

of people through shepherd management and servant leadership.

- **Why Christianity Fails in America.** (2010) ISBN 978-0-9796019-10-- A call for an internal redirection of the heart and soul to make the pristine faith viable in the Twenty-first century.

- **How to Build a Better Spouse Trap.** (2010) ISBN 978-1—9354344-50 – A major failure of faith-based groups is they have made little difference in the lives of individuals and their function in the family. How to choose a mate, learn for our mistakes, stay married, and teach others to break the cycle of dysfunctional relationships. The family unit is a microcosm of faith-based behavior.

- **Discipleship.** (2010) ISBN 978-0-9796019-5-8 A revived edition to better explain the process of a believer's lifestyle from conversion (change direction), to discipleship (learning), to apostle (mature enough to be trusted with the message grace.)

- **SO TALES.** (2011) ISBN 978-1-9354345-80 -- Preserving true 240 true stories from the past for the benefit of family and friends.

- **Designing Valid Research.** (2011) ISBN 978-1-9354345-73 – A guide to designing a research proposal and developing a social scientific dissertation.

- **Titanic Lessons.** (2012) ISBN 978-0-9796019-6-5 – An effort to demonstrate that bigger is not necessarily better and that all building of machines, organizations, and institutions must use material that meets the precise requirements of the task. This must be applied to people, process, and functionality of the human element and the mechanics must match the environment.

- **Why Wait Till Sunday?** (2012) ISBN 978-1-935434-27-6-- A renewal plan for older congregations who depended on programs coming down from sectarian authority rather than locally generated ideas and involvement in seven (7) aspects of renewal.
- **Fighting the Amalekites.** (2013) ISBN 978-1-935434-30-6 – The unhealthy addictions, unproductive habits, an uncontrolled tongue are all little "Amalekites"; unless these are destroyed they will become the destroyer. These join the Amalekites that ambush and take advantage of spiritual weaknesses.
- **Remedial and Surrogate Parenting** (2013) ISBN 978-1-9354344-81--Children are a gift of God and a legacy of faith-based families; therefore, parenting skills are an essential aspect of religion. This work is guidance for remedial human development (0-20) for parents, teachers, and childcare workers.
- **Transformational Leadership in Education.** (2013) Second Edition ISBN 978-1-9354342-38-- A strengths-based approach to education for administrators, teachers, and guidance counselors.
- **Tear Down These Walls.** (2013) ISBN 978-1-9354341-84 -- A priority agenda must be to make people moral citizens of the world before they can become mystical citizens of heaven. Where organized groups choose not to function, personal action could make a difference and break down some of the barriers that divide the faith-based community and strengthen the "One Lord-One Faith–One Baptism" message.
- **The EVERGREEN Devotional New Testament – C.A.F.E. Edition.** (2015, 2018) ISBN 978-1-9354342-69 – EDNT is a 42-year project to translate common NT Greek and determine the meaning

"then" and how words can best be expressed "now" and remain true to the original intent expressed in a common devotional language.

- **Recycled Words n' Stuff.** (2016) ISBN 978-1-9354348-63 – A collection of short narratives and essays of general interest.
- **The Children's Bread – unlocking whole life stewardship** (2018) ISBN 978-1-935434-90-0– *Appreciating faith-based economics and personal wealth to unlock a missional lifestyle and founding for humanitarian and faith-based entities.*
- **Kingdom Growth Through Missional Behavior** (2019)—*adopting the thinking, behaviors, and practices of a missionary in order to globalize the message of grace.* ISBN 978-1-935434-91-7
- **God Has Confidence in You** (2019) ISBN 98-1-950839-04-9. No test has come your way but such as is common to man: God is faithful, who will not permit you to be tested beyond your endurance; but will with each test also show you a way forward, so that you may be victorious.
- **Power of Forgiveness and Reconciliation** (2020) – *Forgiveness is the sunrise of reconciliation.* (2020). ISBN 978-1-950839-06-3
- **Beyond Pulpit, Classroom and Lecture Hall** (2020) — *Unlocking Exposition, Instruction and Research Reporting in Subject Matter Sharing.* ISBN 978-1-950839-03-2
- **Navigating Multiculturalism (2021)** - Orthodox and Orthopraxis Guidance for Sociological Change. ISBN 978-1-950839-10-0

Plus these children's books, in keeping with the Dons of Oxford University:

- **Sleepy Town Lullaby and Story** - (2008)
  ISBN 978-0-9796019-4-1
- **The Scoop about Birthday Soup** - (2008)
  ISBN 978-0-97960198-9

These are available on CD or PDF at present; ebooks in the future:
- The Funky Chicken's Wedding;
- Cranky Not-so-Hottra'
- Cat-Astropic Charlie;
- A Tea Party at Nany's House;
- The Shimonaka Big Drip-per;
- The Mouse of the House;
- The Boy Who Wanted to Grow a Beard;
- The Trouble with Funny Book Cussing;
- The Blue Jay and Grandma's Song;
- Ditala Killed a Dead Snake

Books in Process

Research Methods for Problem Solvers and Critical Thinkers. (2021) —Guidance in development a master's thesis, designing a doctoral research proposal and constructing a defendable dissertation based on social scientific research with an objective of positive social change. ISBN 978-1-935434-92-4

Navigating Multiculturalism - Challenges for Faith-based Groups. (2021) — The wisdom of early thinkers shines a light on the path forward in negotiating community change in a multicultural environment. Knowledge of the past becomes guidelines for future generations: such as, "one never reaches a positive conclusion beginning with a negative premise." A corollary saying remains true "a positive implies a negative." With these two essential presuppositions, one can clearly see the value of common ground and the difficulties with multiple differences. No one can deny the variations of culture, language and tradition which exists in diverse groups. Yet, it is difficult to identify common ground in a pluralistic or multicultural population. Why is this true? ISBN 978-1-950839-13-1

All Believers are Converted Equal (2021) –Developing the Path to Moral Excellence. (Based on 2 Peter Chapter One. ISBN 978-1-950839-11-7

THE POWER SERIES

1. ***Power of Forgiveness and Reconciliation***
   ISBN 978-1-950839-06-3   [2020]
2. **Power of Prayer and Perseverance**
3. **Power of Lordship and Worship**
4. **Power of Giving and Receiving**
5. **Power of Lifestyle and Witness**
6. **Power of Mission and Going**
7. **Power of Fellowship and Friends**
8. **Power of Assimilation and Application**
9. **Power of Learning and Sharing**
10. **Power of Planting and Harvest**
11. **Power of Hunger and Pursuit**
12. **Power of Longevity and Legacy**
13. **Power of Enthusiasm and Affirmation**
14. **Power of Camaraderie and Companions**
15. **Power of Hearth and Home**
16. **Power of Confession and Communion**
17. **Power of Purpose and Timetable**
18. **Power of Faith and Moral Excellence**
19. **Power Scarcity and Abundance**
20. **Power of Connectivity and Friendship**
21. **Power of Love and Hate**

APPENDIX C

The Learning Centre — C.A.F.E.

THE LEARNING CENTRE is a not-for-profit venture to extend the Faith-based services of the sponsoring Faith-based entity to the community and the needs of families and groups in the area, and as such depends on donations from supporters. While businesses rely on sales and governments depend on taxes/appropriations, a nonprofit enterprise is sustained in large part by voluntary contributions. Although THE LEARNING CENTRE receives fees for textbooks, syllabi material, etc., such sources are never enough to operate effective learning programs for biblical, community, and family-based study.

THE LEARNING CENTRE is a moral and intellectual effort, equipping believers to become problem-solvers and effective servant leaders to advance the cause of Christ. THE LEARNING CENTRE is a specialized Faith-based program primarily sponsored by members and friends of the host Faith-based entity. The cost of operation is not charged to students. Friends assist in underwriting the annual operating budget. Donors may assist the operation of THE LEARNING CENTRE by regular donations, just as many do with missional gifts for their place of worship. The Y.E.S. Fund is supported by the generosity of Friends.

Y. E. S. FUNDING

A number of individuals and families share in the Yearly Endowed Security Budget (Y.E.S. Budget) by assisting in the support of the expenses involved in C.A.F.E./A.I.M. studies. THE LEARNING CENTRE invites individuals, businesses, organizations, and families to consider giving to assist Faith-based learning through the Y.E.S. Project that supports the various aspects of the Community and Family programs for the sponsored area. Will you say "YES" to participation and support?

INDIVIDUAL SUPPORT

As an interested individual, I wish to contribute to the Y.E.S. Fund to support the specialized learning opportunities for worthy and serious learners. Here is my [ ] Annual gift of $_____; my [ ] monthly gift of $_____; or my [ ] one-time gift of $_____ to support the work of THE LEARNING CENTRE.

Name_____

Address_____

Telephone (   )_____

Email _____

       Signed: _____

                               Date_____

Contact THE LEARNING CENTRE, PO Box 335, 100 Hendrickson Lane, Bluff City, TN 37618
423-338-9017

AREA CHURCH SPONSORSHIP

THE LEARNING CENTRE would appreciate an opportunity to partner with area local churches and Faith-based groups in training promising young men and women for leadership, community service, and practical ministry roles in the church and community. The Y.E.S. Fund is an excellent opportunity to provide training assistance for young men and women who will become the next level of Faith-based leadership in the community and families of the area. Area Churches are encouraged to sponsor promising local leadership as participants from their congregation who share in the advanced learning opportunities provided?

THE LEARNING CENTRE, PO Box 335,
100 Hendrickson Lane, Bluff City, TN 37618
423-338-9017

BUSINESS AND CORPORATE SPONSORSHIP

Corporate and business operations with a sense of social and community responsibility may contribute to THE LEARNING CENTRE through Y.E.S. Funding or sponsor specific young men and women for these specialized learning opportunities offered by C.A.F.E. or A.I.M. This is a good long-term investment for family and community. Contact THE LEARNING CENTRE, PO Box 335, 100 Hendrickson Lane, Bluff City, TN 37618, 423-338-9017.

C.A.F.E. COMMUNITY AND FAMILY EDUCATION

- Providing faith-based lifestyle training for family life, and practical community service

- C.A.F.E. is a way to reach both the church family and the community with nourishment for mind, soul, and body.

C.A.F.E. is a 4-year program sponsored by a faith-based group to teach devotional reading, community service and practical ministry, through basic New Testament content and practical textbook courses in an informal setting. C.A.F.E. may be used to replace the youth and adult aspects of local education by faith-based groups to better reach families and the community. Although classes will be a "colloquy"—a discussion rather than a taught class, student participation is the objective. Advance preparation by individuals create a C.A.F.E. Class of informed participants ready to learn and share.

The C.A.F.E. logo represents the integration of Biblical study with growth and development classes within the church (the center white square). The larger white square represents the community with C.A.F.E. reaching outside the four walls. The large black square represents the world in which the believers exist as a faith-based entity.

C.A.F.E. ©
COMMUNITY AND FAMILY EDUCATION

Local Sunday school and Christian educational classes for youth training have suffered significant decline in recent decades, it is time for a new approach to community and family education. C.A.F.E. may be an answer to this uncertainty.

Enrollment and Classes

It is time for a new approach to community and family education. C.A.F.E. may be the answer to the decline in local Christian education and classes for youth training. Students will enroll for one year or one term at a time and renew the enrollment based on subject interest and participation. It is time for Sunday school to operate as a "school." Award documentation of completion will be issued each year for those completing three Terms with a Qualification Credential after four years. C.A.F.E. is designed for attendees of the local fellowship and to reach families in the community. It will also develop leadership for the local assembly, strengthen families and equip believers for missional lifestyle witness in the community. Students are enrolled and pay a small fee for books [new community people may receive a "visitor's scholarship" for the first term.] Those enrolled are assigned to read a section of a book or a passage of sacred scripture before coming to class and thereby become an informed participant in class discussion. This has been a major weakness in Sunday school and youth classes; no one but the teacher makes any preparation.

Each class has a leader or mentor (not a lecturer) to guide the discussion relative to the assigned reading. This is an active, participatory and integrated approach to faith-based education where all students feel they are part of the class and may contribute to the learning process. This is a significant step in advancing faith-based education. Also, research has shown that when individuals are "enrolled" they are more apt to attend class; when students make advance preparation, they are more likely to participate. When they pay a small "fee for textbooks, refreshments, etc.," this improves both attendance and participation.

Class Atmosphere of a CAFE

C.A.F.E. is structured to be held in an informal setting; such as, a dining hall, or classroom arranged with tables. The first 15-minutes of class, students should be allowed to have fellowship and quietly eat a snack or drink to create the "CAFE" atmosphere. This will accommodate those who travel a distance or miss a meal to participate. The informal setting should not be permitted to hinder class discussion. The leader should moderate an informal conversation based on the assigned reading. Questions and comments on the assigned reading should be welcomed and encouraged from all students. Discussion should be limited to the area of assigned reading or questions for clarification about material already covered. The leader should make a brief summary of the discussion at the close of the class and remind students of the next reading assignment and scheduled class.

A.I.M./C.A.F.E. Curriculum

Global provides a four-year curriculum structured to prepare young people for volunteerism and community service with non-profits, NGO's and/or faith-based groups who work with children, at-risk-youth, and dysfunctional families. A.I.M./C.A.F.E. curriculum is also designed to develop leadership in the local church and is coached by local leaders. Although classes will be a "colloquy"—a discussion rather than a taught class, student participation is the objective. A.I.M./C.A.F.E. has proved to be an essential source of local educational advancement and adequate training to equip individuals for community service and practical ministry in the most needy areas.

A Service of Global Educational Advance, Inc. (See Nonprofit

OPERATIONAL DELIVERY SYSTEM FOR FAITH-BASED EDUCATION

Normally, religious or faith-based educational efforts are exempt from direct governmental supervision. Notwithstanding, an educational effort delivered by a faith-based entity should provide equal assurance that the facility, curriculum, faculty, and delivery system complies with academic, ethical and operational benchmarks. For example, in a private primary or secondary school using the (K-12) curriculum, students must pass state-sponsored tests to transfer to public or post-secondary schools. Also, denominations have "in-house" training programs to certify or authorize individuals at various levels of service within the sectarian group; such as, deacon, lay minister, approved missionary, licensed pastor, or ordination; such credentialing is without state approval. Yet, when a religious or faith-based group forms a college or seminary that offers degrees with academic nomenclature, they are under direct supervision by the government.

With this in mind Global Educational Advance, Inc. is structuring an educational paradigm shift to assist faith-based groups with innovative educational solutions to meet the religious needs that a totally secular system neglects. This system includes providing religious groups with a faith-based LEARNING CENTRE that consists of a comprehensive ACADEMY with phased in options for a full-scale K-12 primary and/or secondary school or an enhanced "home schooling concept" that uses the ACADEMY as a resource for broader faculty and student socialization. The ACADEMY may be structured as a Student Advanced Tutoring (S.A.T.) Enterprise to prepare public or home-based students to pass standard or required exams. Also the ACADEMY may be offered as an Information Technology (IT) based delivery system via Skype, interactive media similar to missionary or remote population guidance via shortwave radio or limited closed circuit-video where a home-based student or a small group may join a tutor for guidance, enrichment, or a full class session or homebased students may attend special tutoring or socialization sessions with other home-schooled students.

Those entities who choose not to institute a full public Academy may concentrate on the options of support tutoring for public and homebased students who need additional homework guidance or tutoring to pass required standardized grade-level tests or to reach an advanced level of achievement and be prepared for the normal S.A.T. TEST for college entry. Some academies may include:

- D.A.S.H. (Directed Academic Study Helpline) to assist students via telephone or facetime calls.

- H.O.S.T. (Homeschool Official Site for Tutorials and Testing);
- P.U.S.H. (Public Unit Student Assistance) where students in need may receive additional tutoring, coaching, or encouragement to achieve.
- (A.P.T.) Advance Performance Training may be used as part of the S.A.T. Enterprise to prepare students for state standardized tests, or **SAT TEST** for college entrance.

The LEARNING CENTRE includes an Alpha Institute of Ministry (A.I.M.) with a C.A.F.E. curriculum for Community and Family Education that replaces youth and adult church-related Bible study and leadership training with a 4-year plan to teach Bible content and practical courses with approved textbooks/syllabi to equip believers for lifestyle community service and practical ministry. The program of C.A.F.E. may also be used to train leadership for the local church or lay ministers to serve newly formed congregations as part of a church-planting or circuit structure of small groups. Yeshiva Torah Institute is designed as outreach to teach converted Jews the relevant aspects of New Testament Judaism, the Christian lifestyle and both personal and group worship. A full curriculum is available for the Yeshiva.

The LEARNING CENTRE is the umbrella group, the ACADEMY is the K-12 operation with alternative delivery methods, Alpha Institute of Ministry (A.I.M.) is the post-secondary construct and Community and Family Education (C.A.F.E.) is the faith-based curriculum for both faith-based instruction in the normal church education setting and a plan for outreach to families in the community. The options within the LEARNING CENTRE provide opportunities of faith-based groups of all sizes to participate in a comprehensive educational structure with creditable guidance and planned supervision.

Being a member unit (chartered, affiliated, or authorized) of a global system brings authenticity to the local endeavor provides interaction and fellowship with like-minded faith-based educators. This process brings a constructive paradigm shift in disciple-making, lifestyle mentoring, and leadership training for community service and missional living. The adoption of the thinking, behaviors, and practices of a missionary will engage others with the gospel and begin to fulfil the *Believer's Commission:*

> *"19. As you personally go, (going) therefore, and make disciples of all nations, baptizing them in the name of the Father, and of the Son, and of the Holy Spirit: 20. teaching them to observe all things whatever I have commanded you: and behold, I am with you always, even unto the end of the world. Amen." Matthew 28:19, 20 (EDNT).*

CHARTERING AFFILIATED AND AUTHORIZED ENTITIES

The Global AIM Network (*www.globalaim.net*) is designed to present missionaries and global faith-based entities an opportunity to structure a Learning Centre with an Academy (K-12) unit and an educational process that leads to advanced learning through C.A.F.E. (Community and Family Education) and A.I.M. (Alpha Institute of Ministry) to produce family life education, lifestyle guidance, community leadership and practical faith-based community service. This opportunity includes both sacred scriptural content and practical textbook study, written especially to advance faith-based education with individuals and groups outside the normal academic environment. The parent organization, Global Education Advance, Inc., provides structure, guidance, and supervision to assist in both chartering and operating a quality local LEARNING CENTRE through a Network of like-minded individuals.

The Global AIM Network is not designed to qualify individuals for certification or credentials to function outside the realm of practical community and faith-based service. Rather the purpose is to equip faith-based individuals to become moral leaders in local places of worship and become respected citizens to provide practical mentoring and coaching to meet the needs of individuals and families in the community where they live and work.

The Network operates independently from government regulations* but provides equal assurance that a Member entity has complied with a set of academic, ethical and operational benchmarks. The emphasis is on adequate facilities, quality leadership, consistent courses, and practical outcomes in a faith-based environment. Opportunities for professional interaction with individuals involved in similar faith-based efforts are provided by the Network in order to collaborate and develop fair, meaningful and functioning benchmarks for quality faith-based education in areas with limited educational opportunities.

---

* Church and faith-based local educational efforts are normally exempt from government supervision.

The Global AIM Network has as a primary objective to charter, recognize, and encourage quality faith-based educational efforts in the local environment and structure an educational process for continuing practical and quality education where such is not normally available. The Network of local Learning Centers uses approved textbooks and receives guidance from Global Educational Advance, Inc., a nonprofit corporation in Tennessee working to bring transformative and constructive change to communities through various programming for development and continued support for practical education to benefit the young, the disadvantaged, and those who feel a call to missional lifestyle beyond their local community and into global opportunities.

The Network is based in Tennessee but operates with a global vision assisting community-based groups, missionary efforts, NGO's, prison study groups, faith-based educational efforts in local churches, and assistance for youth with potential in their tertiary/post-secondary educational efforts with programs, projects, and services: developing curriculum, textbooks, library and learning resources, and funding.

Presently the Network offers community groups creative programs that produce constructive change in individuals, positive change in family life, spiritual progress in faith-based groups, and positive social change in communities touched by faith-based ministry. The leaders of Global Educational Advance, Inc. and Global AIM Network are experienced educators with credentials and professorial experience in education as well as local, regional, and global educational, ministry, and missional involvement. Their skills and knowledge in many aspects of secondary and post-secondary education, continuing education, home schooling, and faith-based education and ministry are made available to participants in the Network. Additional details may be found on these Internet sites: www.globaledadvance.org, www.gea-books.com and www.globalaim.net [global sites are being updated to include data in this document.] or by correspondence to Global Educational Advance, Inc., 345 Barton Road, Suite 11, Dayton, TN 37321-7635 or greenoxon2@gmail.com.

There are three levels of Membership or Network Affiliation as well as Continued Authorization:

1. Official Chartering for **Probationary Membership** in the Network.
2. After six-months to one (1) year of Probationary Membership, an entity may apply for the **Affiliation** level and ask to be observed and evaluated for meeting minimum benchmark standards for a specific three (3) year endorsement in the chosen aspects of the LEARNING CENTRE programs. This is a service to groups normally not connected with state, regional or national supervision.
3. An entity with Affiliation, may apply for full **Authorization** after an adequate Self-Evaluation Report that includes data on a satisfactory operation for three (3) years. The Network will arrange an official site visit by faith-based academics with supervision experience. With a positive Visit Report, an entity may be granted Authorization for five (5) years.
4. Continued Authorization requires adequate annual reports for five (5) years with continued observation and evaluation throughout the Re-authorizing Process.

5. Entities that fail to meet Network Operational Benchmarks, after adequate warning, may be dropped from Membership or be lowered in status to their level of compliance.
6. Entities dropped from Membership may re-apply after six-months to one (1) year of satisfactory operation.
7. Satisfactory operation includes acceptable facilities, adequate faculty, approved curriculum, satisfactory records, available student outcome data with a record of community service.

Chartering and Authorization is normally a voluntary process that educational entities assume to affirm they meet basic social, educational benchmarks, behave ethically, and employ appropriate quality assurance efforts. The process includes documentation and confirmation of adequate facilities, qualified faculty, competent leadership, participation in community service, and expected student outcomes.

The original Charter and Membership is issued after evaluation of a completed application adequately reviewed by the Network Authorizing Group. Charter and Membership indicates that the educational entity has experienced a detailed peer review. Affiliation means approval of the operation, faculty, curriculum and quality assurance plans. Authorization implies adequate operation, ongoing development, adherence to established benchmarks, adequate student outcomes, and demonstrated advocacy for a stated mission. Note the steps following initial Membership:

1. The process is continued by annual reporting, inspection visits that include an official examination and verification of student records,

institutional documents of teachers, curriculum, and appropriate facilities with scheduled use.

2. A self-evaluation, identifying strengths and weaknesses of the educational process, is both significant and ongoing. The process compares operations and curriculum to established benchmarks and recognizes needed improvements.

3. The self-evaluation process is verified by off-site evaluators who discuss appropriate matters with relevant constituencies.

4. The Network Authorizing Group regularly reviews materials from each Chartered, Affiliated and Authorized entity in accordance with the available educational information to provide a continued level of Membership in the Network.

5. The Network periodically releases via Internet the status of entities based on a Descriptive Report related to the self-evaluation and compliance with identified benchmark standards.

6. Chartered, Affiliated, or Authorized entities may respond to the Descriptive Report and submit additional data to demonstrate further compliance with benchmark standards.

7. Chartered or Affiliated entities may use curriculum, textbooks, and receive minimum guidance from Global Educational Advance, Inc., but the Authorizing Process and the Re-Authorizing reviews are the basis for Membership and the Network's ability to ensure the quality of the operation and learning process offered by Membership entities within the context of their stated mission.

(1)

(1) THE ACADEMY (K-12)

"Helping Every-age Learn Proficiently"

Can you imagine a place where learning differences are a testimony to God's creativity? Can you envision a learning center where children can thrive educationally and develop a love for learning in a safe and caring environment? If you have been searching for an answer to your child's special needs or looking for a school where teachers care for the heart and soul of each student, the Academy may be the answer.

It is not too late, if your son or daughter is struggling in the present learning environment and needs an affordable, specialized learning atmosphere that serves students of all ages regardless of learning difficulties or those simply struggling in school. The Academy will test and evaluate each child and based on an academic and psychological assessment, design a way forward for a significant learning experience.

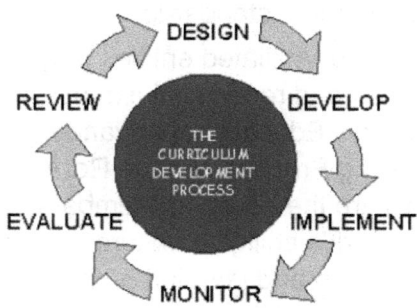

The Curriculum Development Process

The Learning Centre (academy) is a comprehensive class-based school using a K-12 Grammar School concept where adequate education is not available or supervised by a stated authority. Target areas are missionary fields, rural and neglected areas, and inter-city needs. The Academy can be a full (K-12) classroom school; an Internet or Skype delivery system; a Home School support model; or a phased-in model beginning at Primary level age 4-12 and growing to the Secondary level for ages 11-18. The curriculum providing age-appropriate information is only part of the reason students perform well; adapting studies to individual learning styles by teachers with a heart for children is what makes the difference. Most classrooms attempt a one size fits all, but every child learns in his/her own way.

The Academy creates a specialized classroom with an effective learning option personalized to meet the needs of each child. The Academy will assist you to find out why your child is not learning. Can you conceive of a brighter, happier, and more confident child? The Academy tests and customizes the learning experience to the unique abilities of each student. This creates the ideal opportunity for students to learn and excel.

Teaching that is tailored for each student means less stress and more learning, based on a faculty concept the Academy calls **SCAN – Student Concerns Are Normalized** through testing and evaluation. The Academy gives parents a choice with curriculum divided into age-level needs. The age ranges specify the youngest age for a child entering that year and the oldest age for a child leaving that year.

An understanding of the dynamic process of change, growth and interaction in the classroom will assist the teacher in dealing with attentiveness and productivity. A primary task of the teacher is control of the classroom in order to direct the energy of each student in the discovery of the essential elements of the core content covered in the session. It is beneficial to remember that content is not an end in itself; it is a vehicle to transport the student through the learning process. Based on the maturity of the students involved, interaction between students limits their ability to look at and pay attention to the teacher. When this becomes obvious, the teacher feels undervalued which further limits learning. An understanding of this process will assist the teacher in special preparation to maintain the interest, curiosity, and efficiency of the student. Efficiency in learning would mean productivity without loss or waste by each student in the class. The goal is to make each student a moral citizen of society before they can become a mystical citizen of heaven.

CLASSIFICATION OF LEARNING ATTITUDES

Exposition, instruction, and research reporting in subject matter sharing revealed there were no significant differences in speaking whether from a pulpit, in a classroom or a lecture hall. The objectives were clear; accurate and detailed communication. The intent and function of sharing data, information, or facts by speaker and location may be the only definable differences together with many more similarities. Subject matter sharing requires advance preparation, comprehensive knowledge of the subject, and a focus on the venue and the level of participation.

APPENDIX C — THE LEARNING CENTER - C.A.F.E.

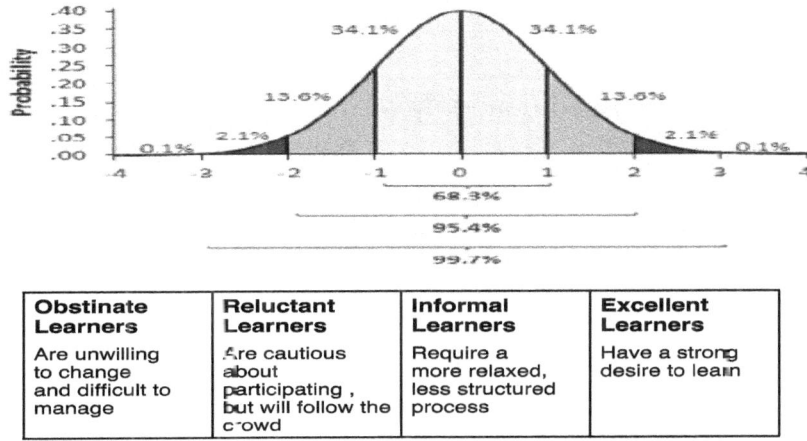

Obstinate Learners	Reluctant Learners	Informal Learners	Excellent Learners
Are unwilling to change and difficult to manage	Are cautious about participating, but will follow the crowd	Require a more relaxed, less structured process	Have a strong desire to learn

Student Attitudes or Predisposition to Learn

Healthy age-specific development together with positive influence from family and friends will produce an excellent student who desires to learn. Teaching such students is almost effortless because they are self-starters. The development of certain personality traits and individual characteristics may produce an informal learner who requires a more relaxed and less structured process for learning. Such students may see things differently than others and develop study and work habits that may not fit the norm. In reality, these students may not receive the highest grades in the class, but they may actually be the better learners with long-term benefits that predict personal and professional achievements.

In some educational systems, the informal learner may be classified as a "C" student but will probably end up owning the business and hiring the excellent "A" students to do the work. A list in history may verify this possibility. Some of the informal learners that ended up on top of the heap were Edison, Lincoln, Einstein, von

Braun, Reagan, Kennedy, Clinton, Bush, and the list goes on and on.

A Faith-based Academy will use the curriculum developed by the governmental entity of the state to prepare students to take the available standard exams and be prepared to seek higher placement. The difference is the quality of instruction and the supportive attitude of the leadership. If the Academy uses the same curriculum as the public schools, so what is the difference? The primary differences are:

1. *All students are tested, assessed, and placed by a specialized system that assists the Academic in placing the student in the proper division and with the proper teacher..*
2. *Teacher attitudes and approach to individual students are based on the above assessment.*
3. *Students are grouped into a common classroom with a specialized teacher and a teaching assistant or teacher's aide.*
4. *No student feels classified or categorized in the group of students, but each work at their own pace guided by the faculty. One student may excel without another feeling left behind. Individual differences are handled one-on-one by the teacher and not as a class.*
5. *Students are permitted to advance at their own pace and may be moved to the next higher-level class whenever the teacher feels they are ready to perform adequately at the next level. Advancement or promotion to the next level class is a judgment call of the present teacher. When "excellent" work at one level adequately predicts good performance at the next level, a student is advanced. Such "any time" advancement becomes an encouragement for others to excel.*

6. All students are placed in one of three primary levels or one of three secondary levels. These levels are shown below and provide for a range of ages and academic levels to provide a "comfort index" in the affective domain and a "learning index" in the cognitive domain. This is the opposite of "main streaming" where individual students feel out of place; it clearly places a student in a learning group where they may receive individual attention and progress at their own pace.
7. The process creates a learning environment where individuals learn from each other and develop individual study skills and participate in group learning exercises. The grouping of the students is a specialized aspect of the Academy and is believed to be the basis for an excellent learning environment.

The Difference in Learning is Primarily the Teacher

Learning in theory is both intellectual and rational. In reality, the educational process is a highly emotional and interpersonal practice and requires a combination of intellectual excitement and interpersonal rapport. There must be an empathy relationship between teacher and learner. This is a trust relationship with firm reliance on the integrity and ability of the teacher and a concern for learning expressed by the student. The faculty directed learning model works only with integrity and trust.

Gregory's Laws of Teaching: In 1846 John Milton Gregory gave up the study of law to become a Baptist minister and then a college teacher and administrator, working primarily in Michigan and Illinois, where he organized the University of Illinois. *The Seven Laws of Teaching* were clearly expressed in Gregory's book by that title published in 1884. These are timeless insights that remain useful. One who understands these basic rules will receive the praise of grateful students. Neglect these fundamentals and one's teaching credentials and even subject-specific certification will be useless pieces of paper. Those who attempt to teach without Gregory's perspective will become frustrated and produce a class of passive and even resistant pupils. What does "pupil" mean? From the Latin it describes a "little boy" or a "little doll." It suggests a place of immaturity. Teachers who do not effectively teach contribute to the immaturity of a generation and may be responsible for many of the problems that society has to face because of immature judgment and/or acts of undisciplined individuals.

In the simplest form, **Gregory's Laws of Teaching** are still relevant to the needs of learners.

1. *The teacher must know that which he/she would teach.*
2. *A learner is one who attends with interest to the lesson.*
3. *The language, used as a medium between teacher and learner, must be common to both.*
4. *The facts to be taught must be learned through facts already known.*
5. *Excite and direct the self-activity of the pupils, as a rule telling them nothing that they can learn on their own.*
6. *The pupil must reproduce in his/her own words the facts to be learned. Memorization is the first level of learning. After the facts of the lesson are clear there is an elementary degree of understanding. The next step in the process is the ability to paraphrase a thought or concept in one's own words. Finally, the desire to search for supportive*

evidence to support one's understanding is realized, and an effort made to apply what was learned. Application is required to reinforce the learning process.

7. At least one-third of teaching/study/class time should be given to review and/or application of the lessons learned

Affective Direction in Teaching: A basic assumption in education is that student behavior and achievement are governed by affective well-being. Understanding the affective domain provides useful information for those who guide students in personal growth and academic development. To improve the knowledge of the affective domain in learning, a planning and teaching model with general application is needed. A scheme for classifying and organizing instructional material will chart the scope and sequence of instruction. An instructional design based on developmental theory could provide the tools and a sense of direction that makes it possible for teachers to prepare and implement instructional goals.

Teaching goals need to assist the learner in recognizing and understanding emotions, attitudes, values, and how their surroundings and associations with others influence what they say and do. The teaching goals should make students aware of the outcomes and consequences that may result from feelings of joy, anger, fear, surprise, or distress. Teachers need to teach students to weigh the outcome of decisions with reference to the effect decisions may have on them and others and recognize the different ways that they could respond. Finally, students must understand the nature, forms, and consequences of aggression and apply their knowledge of emotions, attitudes, and values toward positive, real-life experience.

An effective teaching model will assist the student with self-concept, interpersonal relationship with classmates, and how they feel about the learning environment. This aesthetic sensitivity determines, to a large extent, the degree of motivation the student has to achieve an educational objective. Proceeding from the known and accepted, a synthesis of models may be used in plotting a course that leads to planning and teaching in both the cognitive and affective domains. This means planning and teaching for thinking and feeling dealing with both the cognitive and the affective domains.

The EVERGREEN Devotional New Testament
C.A.F.E. EDITION
Community And Family Education©

(I) Individual and/or Family Devotional Readings

Evening and Morning

> *And God called the light Day, and the darkness He called night: and **the evening and the morning were the first day.** (Genesis 1:5)*

The early congregations did not have a copy of the New Testament but received and read aloud each book or letter as it was written.

"And when this letter is read among you, send it to be read also in the assembly of the Laodiceans, and that you likewise read the letter from Laodicea." (Colossians 4:16)

It is suggested the EDNT be read devotionally by individuals and/or families chronologically by books, reading one or more Topic Sections in each Chapter each evening and morning. The OT process was to rest *from* labor, but the NT order is to rest *for* the coming labor. This is why devotions should begin each evening as one prepares for the next day and each morning *for a fresh start* for the day.

Note the approximate NT Chronological Order:

Written during AD45 — AD60

The General Letter of James
The Gospel According to Mark
The First Letter to the Thessalonians
The Second Letter to the Thessalonians
The Letter to the Galatians
The First Letter to the Corinthians
The Second Letter to the Corinthians
The Letter to the Romans
The Gospel According to Luke
The Gospel According to Matthew

Written during AD61 – AD68

The Letter to Philemon
The Letter to the Colossians
The Letter to the Ephesians
The Letter to the Philippians
The Acts of the Apostles

The First Letter to Timothy
The Letter to Titus
The First Letter of Peter
The General Letter of Jude
The Letter to the Hebrews
The Second Letter of Peter
The Second Letter to Timothy

Written during AD 85 — AD95

The Gospel According to John
The First Letter of John
The Second Letter of John
The Third Letter of John
The Revelation of John

Providing Practical Bible Study, Lifestyle Training
for Family Life, Community Service,
And Faith-based Personal Ministry.

[II] Bible Study Track: C.A.F.E. NT Bible Content Study

Using The EVERGREEN Devotional New Testament

[Usually under A.I.M.]

(May be used as a part of the A.I.M. Study and/or to replace Sunday Literature for Youth and Adults)

C.A.F.E. CURRICULUM AND TEXT

"...cutting straight the word of truth."

Text: *The EVERGREEN Devotional New Testament* *

*See *Quick Reference* pp 433 for Traditional and Alphabetical New Testament Order.

C.A.F.E. Enrollment and Classes

Sunday school and youth training have suffered significant decline in recent decades, it is time for a new approach to community and family education. C.A.F.E. is a 4-year program sponsored by a faith-based group to teach practical ministry, community service and basic New Testament content in an informal setting. It can be used to replace the youth and adult aspects of education by faith-based groups to better reach families and the community. Students will enroll one year/or one term at a time and renew the enrollment based on interest and participation. Certificates of completion will be issued each year for those completing three Terms with a Qualification Document after four years.

C.A.F.E. is designed for families in the community and to develop leadership for the local church, strengthen families, and equip believers for faith-based lifestyle service in the community. C.A.F.E. Bible Study Track: (1) Enrollment/sign-up day/ 16 Weeks/; (2) One class break for prayer an reflection/16 Weeks/(3) One class break for prayer and reflection/16 Weeks/ (4) Final class prayer and reflection. 1/16/1/16/1/16/1=52 Weeks. Students will enroll for one year that includes three Terms of 16 weeks. The class will be a "colloquy"—a formal discussion rather than a taught class; student participation is the objective. Students will read the assigned chapter(s) in the EVERGREEN Devotional New Testament (EDNT) before coming to class in order to be an informed participant in discussion.

Advance Reading Assignment prior to first class: Each student should have their own copy of the EDNT (Hardcover, Softcover or eBook). Read the front and back material which explains why the author believed it was necessary to develop a devotional text from the original Greek and change the chronological order and grouping of books to better see the progressive development revealed in the New Testament.

I. <u>Freshmen Year</u> — Learning Leader should group short chapters and divide long chapters to make 48 lesson, with 4 Sessions for prayer and reflection.

Narratives about the Life of Jesus —EDNT
- **Term One** —Mark (16 chapters)
- **Term Two** —Matthew 1—28
  - Lesson 1   Matthew 1—2:15
  - Lesson 2   Matthew 2:16—7-12
  - Lesson 3   Matthew 7-13—12:45
  - Lesson 4   Matthew 12:46– 15:20
  - Lesson 5   Matthew 15:21—18:20
  - Lesson 6   Matthew 18:21 –19:30
  - Lesson 7   Matthew 20:1—22:14
  - Lesson 8   Matthew 22:15 –23-36
  - Lesson 9   Matthew 23:37 –25:46
  - Lesson 10   Matthew 26:1 –27:44
  - Lesson 11   Matthew 27:45 –28:20

- Lessons 12-16 John chapters 1-5
- **Term Three** — Remaining 16 chapters of John.

II. <u>Sophomore Year</u> — Learning Leader should group short chapters and divide long chapters to make 48 lesson, with 4 Sessions for prayer and reflection.

Letters to Theophilus — EDNT

- **Term One:** Luke 1-16
- **Term Two:** Luke 17-24 and Acts 1-8
- **Term Three:** Acts 9-28 [29] [leader will have to double up on 5 chapters]

III. <u>Junior Year</u> — Learning Leader should group short chapters and divides long chapters to make 48 lessons, with 4 Sessions for prayer and reflection.

Letters to Assembled Believers — EDNT

- **Term One:** [I Thessalonians (5) II Thessalonians (3), Galatians (6), [2 extra classes for general discussion and review]
- **Term Two:** I Corinthians (16) II Corinthians (12) [group chapters to complete16 weeks]
- **Term Three:** Romans (16)

IV. <u>Senior Year</u> — Learning Leader should group short chapters and divide long chapters to make 48 Lesson, with 4 Sessions for prayer and reflection.

Letters to Assembled Believers continued — EDNT

- **Term One:** Colossians (4) Ephesians (6) Philippians (4)

Relational Letters —EDNT

- **Term Two:** Philemon (1), First Timothy (6), Titus (3), Second Timothy (4), Second John (1), Third John (1)

Letters to Scattered Believers — EDNT

- **Term Three:** Leader will have to group chapters for discussion to complete in 16 Weeks.
  - Class 1- James (4 chapters),
  - Class 2- First Peter (5 chapters),
  - Class 3 - Hebrews chapters 1-3
  - Class 4 - Hebrews chapters 4-6
  - Class 5 - Hebrews chapters 7-10
  - Class 6 - Hebrews chapters 11-13
  - Class 7 - Second Peter (3),
  - Class 8 - Jude (1),
  - Class 9 - First John (5),
  - Class 10- Revelation pp 381-384,
  - Class 11- Revelation pp 385-388,
  - Class 12- Revelation pp 389-392,
  - Class 13- Revelation pp 393-396
  - Class 15- Revelation pp 401-404
  - Class 16 -Revelation pp 405-406

C.A.F.E. Study Tracks

[III] Class Textbook Track: C.A.F.E. Classes
Using various textbooks in a local faith-based

Alpha Institute of Ministry (AIM)
Local C.A.F.E. CURRICULUM AND TEXT

"a workman unashamed"

Leadership may move textbooks into different terms when current priorities exist. Additional text may be received through <u>www.gea-books.com.</u>

FIRST YEAR TEXTBOOKS: Learning Leader groups short chapters and divides long chapters to make 16 lessons.

TERM ONE – 16 Weeks – Spiritual Progress Priorities

- 1-12—<u>God's work Done God's Way</u> —*You don't have to make headlines to make a difference.*
- 1-4 sections—<u>Discipleship</u> – *A vital aspect of Christian living*

TERM TWO – 16 Weeks –Listening and Learning

- 2-6 only -<u>Interpreting and Author's Words</u>—*Refine study and writing by understand the written word*
- 1-12 <u>Beyond Pulpit, Classroom, and Lecture Hall</u> –*Unlocking Exposition, Instruction, and Research Reporting in Subject Matter Sharing*

TERM THREE – 16 Weeks –Marriage, Family, and Parenting

- 1-12—<u>How to Build a Better Spouse Trap</u>—*Choose a mate, stay married, overcome dysfunctional behavior*
- 1-9—<u>Remedial and Surrogate Parenting</u>—*Like footprints each child is different*

SECOND YEAR TEXTBOOKS: Learning Leader groups short chapters and divide long chapters to make 16 lessons.

TERM ONE – 16 Weeks –Leadership in Education

- 1-12 —<u>Transformational Leadership in Education</u> – *Strengths-based Approach to Change*

TERM TWO – 16 Weeks –Spiritual Warfare and Faith-based Behavior

- 1-8—<u>Fighting the Amalekites</u>—*Destroy the things that would destroy you*
- 1-10—<u>Navigating the Challenges of Faith-based Behavior</u>— *Conduct that Exhibits a Moral Course in Life*

TERM THREE – 16 Weeks –Renewal and Relationship Problems

- 1-12 <u>Power of Forgiveness and Reconciliation</u> – *Forgiveness is the sunrise of reconciliation*
- 1-6 only—<u>Why Wait till Sunday?</u>—*A plan for local renewal and evangelism*

THIRD YEAR TEXTBOOKS: Learning Leader groups short chapters and divide long chapters to make 16 lessons.

TERM ONE – 16 Weeks – Beyond Name Brand Religion

- 1-16—<u>Tear Down These Walls</u>—*Beyond freeze frame thinking and name brand religion*

TERM TWO – 16 Weeks – Lifestyle Behavior

- 1-12—<u>Accessing The Children's Bread</u> –*Unlocking a Missional Lifestyle and Funding for Faith-based Entities*

TERM THREE – 16 Weeks –Developing a Relational Congregation

- 1-12 —<u>Kingdom Growth Through Missional Behavior</u> –*Adopting the thinking, behaviors, and practices of a missionary in order to globalize the gospel*
- 1-9—<u>Titanic Lessons</u>—*Relationship problems for a growing church*

FOURTH YEAR TEXTBOOKS: Learning Leader groups short chapters and divide long chapters to make 16 lessons.

TERM ONE – 16 Weeks – The Faith Dynamics

- 1-10 + A1-A7 — <u>Discipling Middle Eastern Believers</u> – *Understanding other Religions with Cultural Differences*

TERM TWO — 16 Weeks – Respect for Aging

- 1-10 – <u>Ageing has a Silver Lining</u> – *Coping with rainy days*

TERM THREE – 16 Weeks – Evangelism and Church Growth

- 1-5 sections — <u>Why Churches Die</u> — *A guide to basic evangelism and church growth*
- 1-12 — <u>Why Christianity Fails</u> — *Making faith viable in the Twenty-first century*

TERM, FOUR – 16 WEEKS – Servant Leadership

- 1-10 — <u>Sympathetic Leadership Cybernetics</u> — *Serving through shepherd management/servant leadership*
- 1-18 — <u>Walking With Miss Kay</u> — *A Believer's Journey to Glorify God*

Global will recommend substitute text for any listed textbook not considered appropriate to the local needs.

Award documentation of completion will be issued each year for those completing the Term offered, with a Qualification Document after four years:

- Certificate Templates for each year completed and for the final
- Qualification Document when all four years are completed.
- Available at <u>www.gea-books.com</u> or email <u>greenoxon2@gmail.com</u>

APPENDIX D

Bible in Public Schools

In 1949-50 I was fortunate, as part of my History Major, to take two courses at Chattanooga High School sponsored by this program. It was a neutral foundation designed to provide cultural literacy and equip students to contribute to a global society. The courses gave me a perspective that greatly influenced my life.

(https://BibleInTheSchools.com/1.53/about)

Bible History elective classes in the public schools are an opportunity for students to have a viewpoint neutral, foundational study – at no cost to taxpayers – of one of the cornerstone texts of world history, which helps students become culturally literate and better equipped to thrive and contribute to a global world.

- **Entering the 98th year** - Bible History elective courses have been a gift from the community to public school youth since 1922. Charitable donations to Bible in the schools cover the complete costs of running a Bible History elective course program for middle and high school students in Hamilton County, Tennessee. For the 2019-2020 academic year, Bible History elective courses will be offered in 27 schools and are available to students in grades 6-12.
- **Students** - 4,536 students completed Bible History elective courses during the 2018-2019 academic year. This is an increase of 12% over the previous year.

- **No Tax Dollars** - Bible History classes are funded in entirety by the generosity of the community through voluntary charitable contributions. Annually, Hamilton County Schools and participating Charter Schools are reimbursed for the complete costs of the program.

- **Court Approved** - In 1980, a federal court affirmed that teaching the Bible in public school is constitutionally permissible. The curriculum is court approved and meets legal requirements. The federal Judge affirmed the Bible will be the textbook.

- **25 Teachers** - highly credentialed teachers are selected and hired by school principals. Instructional leadership and administrative oversight of all teachers is conducted by Hamilton County Department of Education's Program Coordinator, Bible History (Dr. Matt Johnson). These individuals bring strong pedagogy to Hamilton County Schools and collectively hold 60 degrees. All are funded by charitable donations to Bible in the Schools.

- All Hamilton County Bible History teachers are required to be certified by the State of Tennessee. They are college/university trained educators who also hold a minimum of 12 official college-level Bible content credit hours. All courses are required to be direct studies of books of the Bible. The 25 teachers for the 2019-2020 academic year, including the Bible History Program Coordinator, are strongly credentialed and collectively hold 60 degrees. 36% of the teachers have Seminary degrees.

- Bible History teachers are funded entirely through private contributions from local individuals, businesses, faith-based entities, and foundations. No tax dollars are used to fund this for-credit, elective for public school students. Hamilton County Schools will be reimbursed in July 2019 for a projected $1.5 million for the complete costs of the county-wide Bible History program in 25 schools during the 2018-2019 school year. Included in reimbursement costs are: teacher salaries, all benefits, taxes, classroom supplies, ongoing teacher professional development, and the costs of a full-time Bible History Program Coordinator.

Observable Change - Teachers report observable changes in student attitude, behavior, and outlook as a result of taking a Bible History course.

Courses Offered - Courses are academically rigorous, for-credit, and are voluntary electives. Courses offered:

- Genesis - 6th Grade
- Exodus - 7th Grade
- Life of Jesus - 8th Grade (Based on book of Luke)
- Old Testament Survey - 9th, 10th, 11th, 12th Grade
- New Testament Survey - 9th, 10th, 11th, 12th Grade

Textbook - The textbook used is the Bible

2018-2019 PRE/POST TEST AVERAGES REFLECT 127% INCREASE IN BIBLE CONTENT KNOWLEDGE COUNTY-WIDE

Bible History classes in public schools would not be possible without broad community support. Classes are:

- **Welcomed by the local education community.** Bible History is offered as an elective, only by principals who request to add this course offering as part of their overall academic curriculum. Past data suggests 70% percent of students who attend schools that offer Bible History will elect at least one course while at that school.

- **Sustained by a loyal, growing and diverse donor base,** who have generously gifted Bible History elective courses for over 97 years.
- **Promoted by** an active board that includes 32 prominent leaders from throughout Hamilton County.

More data: (https://BibleInTheSchools.com/1.53/about)

BIBLIOGRAPHY

Babbie, Earl. (2001). *The practice of social research* (9th edition) Wadsworth/Thompson Learning.

Balloo, Paratan (2018). *Leadership Theory & Social Change --Formal and Informal Aspects of Leadership in Organizations.* Nashville: GlobalEdAdvancePress.

Berger, R.M., & Patchner, M.A. (1988). *Planning for research: a guide for the helping professions.* Newbury Park, CA: Sage.

Behrens, L. (1992). *The American Experience: A Sourcebook for Critical Thinking and Writing.* Boston: Allyn and Bacon.

Bloom B. S. (1956). *Taxonomy of Educational Objectives, Handbook I: The Cognitive Domain.* New York: David McKay Co Inc.

Brockett, R. G. and Hiemstra, R. (1991) *Self-Direction in Adult Learning: Perspectives on Theory, Research, and Practice,* London and New York: Routledge.

Bryman, Alan. (2008). **Social Research Methods**. Oxford University Press.

Candy, Philip C. 1991. *Self-Direction for Lifelong Learning.* San Francisco:

Green, Hollis Lynn (2008). *Interpreting An Author's Words,* Nashville: GlobalEdAdvancePress.

Crosby, B.C. (1999). *Leadership for Global Citizenship: Building Transnational Community.* Thousand Oaks, CA: Sage Publications.

Drucker, F. Peter. (1995). *Managing in a Time of Great Change.* New York: Penguin Group.

Glaser, Edward M. (1941). *An Experiment in the Development of Critical Thinking.* Volmnis zu.

Giles, C. (2006). *Transformational Leadership in Challenging Urban Elementary Schools: A role For Parental Involvement?* University of Buffalo, The State University of New York.

Green, Hollis L. (2007) *Sympathetic Leadership Cybernetics,* GlobalEdAdvancePress. Nashville.

Green, Hollis L. (2007) *Why Christianity Fails in America,.* GlobalEdAdvancePress. Nashville.

Green, Hollis L. (2009) .*Remedial and Surrogate Parenting* GloblEdAdvancePress. Nashville.

Green, Hollis L. (2019). *The Evergreen Devotional New Testament C.A.F.E. Edition*, Post-Gutenberg Books. Nashville.

Green, Hollis L. (2010). *Designing Valid Research.*, GlobalEdAdvancePress. Nashville.

Green, Hollis L. and Swanson, G. A. (2021), *Research Methods for Problem Solvers and Critical Thinkers,* USA GlobalEd AdvancePRESS. Nashville.

Gutek, Gerald Lee, (1988). *Philosophical And Ideological Perspectives on Education*, Prentice Hall

Hall, Edward T., *The Silent Language.* (1973) Anchor Books Edition:

Hamby, B.W. (2007). *The Philosophy of Anything: Critical Thinking in Context.* Dubuque, Iowa. Kendall Hunt Publishing Company.

Hammond M, Collins R (1991). *Self-directed learning: Critical Practice.* Kogan Page.

Israel, M. and Hay, I. (2006) *Research Ethics for Social Scientists: Between Ethical Conduct and Regulatory Compliance.* London: Sage.

Kenneth D. Bailey (2006). *Living systems theory and social entropy theory.* Systems Research and Behavioral Science, 22, 291-300.

Leithwood, K. (Ed.) (2000). *Understanding schools as intelligent systems.* CT: JAI Press

McLuhan, Marshall (1967). *The Medium is the Message.* London: Allen Lane

Miller, James Grier, (1978). *Living Systems.* New York: McGraw-Hill.

O'Toole, James (1995). *Leading Change: Overcoming the Ideology of Comfort and The Tyranny of Custom.* San Francisco: Jossey-Bass Publishers.

Pohl, Michael. (1999). *Learning to Think, Thinking to Learn: Models and Strategies to Develop a Classroom Culture of Thinking.* Hawker Brownlow Ed.

Ruane, Janet. M. (2004). *Essentials of Research Methods: A Guide to Social Science Research.* Blackwell.

Schaller, Lyle. (1972). *The Change Agent.* Nashville: Abingdon.

Seech, Zachary (2005), *Open Minds and Everyday Reasoning*, 2nd Edition. Belmont, CA: Wadsworth/Thomson Learning.

Shook, John. (2000). *Dewey's Empirical Theory of Knowledge and Reality.* The Vanderbilt Library of American Philosophy.

Sleeper, R.W. (2001). *The Necessity of Pragmatism: John Dewey's Conception of Philosophy.* Introduction by Tom Burke. University of Illinois Press.

Swanson, G.A. and Miller, James Grier. (1989) *Measurement and interpretation in Accounting: A Living Systems Theory Approach.* New York: Qurum Books.

Swanson, G.A., and Green, Hollis L. (1991, 2004). *Understanding Scientific Research: An Introductory Handbook for the Social Professions.* Nashville: Oxford/ACRSS Press.

White, Alasdair A. K. (2008). *From Comfort Zone to Performance Management.* White & MacLean Publishing.

Wlodkowski, R. J. (1998). *Enhancing Adult Motivation to Learn.* San Francisco, Jossey-Bass Publications.

ONLINE RESOURCES

- Online International Journals Research methods knowledge database: http://www.socialresearchmethods.
- Resource for methods in evaluation in social research. http://gsociology.icaap.org/methods/
- Research methods and statistics arena. http://www.researchmethodsarena.com/resources/
- Quantitative and Qualitative Analysis in Social Sciences http://www.qass.org.uk/
- Social Research Update. http://sru.soc.surrey.ac.uk/
- Survey Research Methods. http://w4.ub.uni-konstanz.de/srm/

Beyond the credentials, certification and consistency of the speaker is the integrity and character of the presenter. This is apart from the functional duties of the position.

A judgement by the listener, as to the moral authority, character and authenticity of the presenter, is an assigned value to the language and structure of the performance and the reliability of the presenter.

Logical audience questions are:
- Who are you?
- Why are you here?
- What qualifies you to speak on this?

Beyond the subject matter sharing is the person, their position, personality and personal trustworthiness.

Be eager to present yourself
approved to God,
a workman unashamed,
cutting straight the word of truth."

(2 Timothy 2:15 EDNT)

www.ingramcontent.com/pod-product-compliance
Lightning Source LLC
Chambersburg PA
CBHW050640170426
43200CB00008B/1089